A HUMAN'S GUIDE
FOR
EVERYDAY LIFE

*KNOWLEDGE AND KNOW-HOW
CONCENTRATE,
FOR THOSE WHO WANT TO DO*

A HUMAN'S GUIDE FOR EVERYDAY LIFE

*KNOWLEDGE AND KNOW-HOW
CONCENTRATE,
FOR THOSE WHO WANT TO DO*

ERIC J. SYVERSON
AKA
ABDULQAWI YUSUF IBN DALE

ATTENTION

This book contains the author's beliefs, experiences, and hypotheses concerning various aspects of life. Health, capability, and understanding vary; therefore, the author cannot and does not guarantee acting on the information in this book will lead to positive outcomes and cannot and does not guarantee acting on the information in this book will not result in negative outcomes. The consumer of this information is solely responsible for his or her choices, actions, and ensuing results. Please be reasonable, responsible, and careful.

Copyright © 2019 Eric J. Syverson
All rights reserved

READ THE AUTHOR'S AUTOBIOGRAPHY, IN VERSE, AT:
www.ahumansguide.com

QUESTIONS? COMMENTS? CONTACT US AT:
ejs@ahumansguide.com

LIKE THIS BOOK? WRITE A REVIEW AT:
www.amazon.com

CONTENTS

THE OPENING..1

MAJOR THEMES PRIMER...3

1. SHREWD WISDOM FOR EVERYDAY LIFE...............................5

2. A HUMAN'S GUIDE TO RICHES..21

3. CHARISMATIC INFLUENCE..27

4. LEARNING EFFICIENCY HABITS...35

5. HEALTHY RELATIONSHIPS..51

6. WARFARE LEADERSHIP..63

7. GOVERNING JUSTLY..69

8. INVITING HUMANITY TO SUCCESS.......................................75

9. FOR MUSLIM EYES ONLY: UNIFYING OUR MUSLIM WORLD........79

THE CLOSING..83

THE OPENING

In the name of Allah, the Compassionate, the Merciful

Praise be to Allah, the Lord of the worlds. The Compassionate, the Merciful, Master of the Day of Judgement. You alone we worship and You alone we ask for help. Guide us on the straight path. The path of those You favored, not those who earned Your anger, and not those who went astray.

—The Qur'an 1:1-7 (translation)

This book is aspirational
Not yet mastered
Who I want to be
Not yet who I am
My knowledge and know-how to date
Neither genetic nor instinctive
Rather, observed, experienced, and learned
Here we go
Some already know how to do
And do very well
Others don't know how to do
So they don't
The foolish and dangerous don't know how to do
But do anyway
Shame on the one who knows how to do
But is too scared to

EJS 25 Rabee'ulAwwal 1441 (22 November 2019)

A HUMAN'S GUIDE FOR EVERYDAY LIFE

A HUMAN'S GUIDE FOR EVERYDAY LIFE: MAJOR THEMES PRIMER

Certainly, those who say our Lord is Allah, then stay on the straight path, they will neither fear nor grieve. They are the companions of Paradise, living therein forever, their reward for their (good) deeds.

—The Qur'an 46:13-14 (translation)

What we do and don't do defines who we are, what we accomplish, and how we're remembered. Though we'd all say we want what's best for ourselves, our family, and our society, our actions often prove otherwise. This book is a guide explaining what we must do to be successful, why we must do it, and how to do it. It covers happiness, health, wealth, status, learning, efficiency, excellence, influence, leadership, war, relationships, love, sex, religion, and politics. If we practice its truths, then we'll be the best human beings we can be; if we don't, then we'll underachieve. The following is an overview of this book's key takeaways:

- Define our principles, then make them reality.

- Do what gets us what we want and avoid what doesn't.

- Don't let anyone take advantage of us or force us to do what we don't want to.

- Renounce fear, softness, and weakness in favor of toughness, bravery, and martyrdom.

- Be confident, self-assured, and go after what we want.

- Aspire for what's natural, simple, and doable.

- Concentrate our resources and divide our rivals, attack with distraction then surprise.

- Be prepared, precise, and persistent.

- Make people feel how we want them to feel, believe what we want them to believe, and want to do what we want them to do.

- Make connections, care about others, develop meaningful relationships, and don't be selfish.

- Always be on the lookout for dangers and opportunities.

- Freedom is our default setting.

- Forgive ourselves, be optimistic, and never lose hope.

1
SHREWD WISDOM FOR EVERYDAY LIFE

Whoever desires honor, power, and glory, all honor, power, and glory are with Allah. To Him good words ascend and good deeds He exalts, but those plotting evil will receive a severe punishment, and their plots will perish.

—The Qur'an 35:10 (translation)

CONSISTENCY

DEFINE WHO YOU WANT TO BE, THEN BE THAT PERSON

We need a firm sense of identity, a purpose driving our daily actions, and to feel our lives have significant meaning; committing to, and living consistently with, a set of life-guiding principles (beliefs, values, and goals) provides the identity, purpose, and meaning we need for satisfying lives. A firm sense of identity originates from sincerely held beliefs explaining who we are, where we come from, how we got here, where we need to go, and how to get there; our beliefs define how the world is supposed to work and inspire who we want to be. A purpose which drives our daily actions comes from the value system derived from our beliefs; our values are our beliefs put into practice, the do's and don'ts of who we want to be. Feeling our lives have significant meaning springs from pursuing, as a group member, the goal of making our beliefs and values benefit the external world; this makes us feel connected to a broader whole that's working for something greater than ourselves; we become part of a rightly guided community shaping the world how it should be. Our principles are who we aspire to be, but our actions make us who we truly are; to feel comfortable, who we aspire to be and who we truly are must be consistent. When our actions are consistent with our principles, our need for identity, purpose, and meaning is satisfied; making us feel content, driven, and important; while not having principles, or living inconsistently with them, leaves us feeling lost and confused, tense and anxious, guilty and empty. Too many of us live without principles, and too many of us don't live up to the principles we have; this is the main reason so many of us feel dissatisfied with our lives and is the main source of many of our health problems. Establish principles by first defining our beliefs: open our hearts and minds up to the truth; observe, critique, and contemplate the external world, history, and other belief systems; then commit to the worldview (origin story, definitions of right and wrong, final destination) we believe is true: don't settle for convenience, sacrifice for truth. Next, adopt the values associated with these beliefs, and at all times, in all places, and under all circumstances, act consistently with them: make our lifestyle and our values match. Now, develop our vision for making our beliefs and values positively impact the external world; form or join groups dedicated to this vision; and make this vision's realization our life's goal, mission, and passion.

ADVANTAGE

DO WHAT GETS YOU WHAT YOU WANT AND AVOID WHAT DOESN'T

Understanding advantage is understanding human behavior. All our decisions, both conscious and subconscious, are motivated by our pursuit of perceived advantage (gaining, increasing, and protecting desirables); we're attracted to, and pushed into action by, what we believe will benefit us. If we feel an action helps us gain a desirable (health, wealth, love, safety, status, and pleasure) then we want to do it, if we feel an object increases our collection of desirables then we want to own it, and if we feel the ownership of any of our current desirables is threatened then we're doubly motivated to protect it. The pursuit of perceived advantage manifests itself through conscious decisions (contemplating and debating, then selecting what we believe is the best choice) and subconscious pressures (cravings, desires, and impulses pushing us towards action). The problem with our pursuit of advantage is not everything we perceive to be advantageous truly is; drug addicts, self-mutilators, and child molesters all believe, either consciously or subconsciously, they are pursuing their advantage. Following our heart, gut, or instincts isn't enough: we must willfully define for ourselves what's advantageous and what's not. When we define for ourselves what's advantageous and what's not, we clearly know what to do and what not to do; but when we don't define for ourselves what's advantageous and what's not, we could misinterpret thrills and excitement, selfishness, evil desires, and exploitation of others as advantage. No matter how badly we want, crave, or desire something, anything harming us or making us terrible, loathsome, disgusting human beings is disadvantageous. Classify actions consistent with our principles as advantageous, actions inconsistent with our principles as disadvantageous, then act to our advantage: do what gets us what we want and avoid what doesn't; make things happen when, where, and how we want them to; control our emotions, desires, and impulses; and never accept bad deals.

CONCENTRATION

MATCH YOUR CONCENTRATED RESOURCES AGAINST YOUR OPPONENT'S DIVIDED RESOURCES

The most doesn't win, the most at the right place and time wins. Concentration (united groups, consolidated wealth, focused attention) is strength and division (individuals, fractured groups, modest wealth, scattered attention) is weakness. Concentrated resources beat divided resources: united groups defeat individuals and fractured groups, big money beats little money, and focused attention beats scattered attention. Optimize outcomes by matching our concentrated resources against our opponent's divided resources. When we match our concentration against our opponent's division, we win; but when we don't concentrate our resources, or we don't divide our opponent's resources, outcomes are uncertain. Never leave outcomes to chance, guarantee advantage through our concentration and our opponent's division. In all we do, be concentrated, divide rivals, and match our concentrated resources against opponent's divided resources: concentrate, split adversary, then strike.

TEAMWORK

COOPERATE, COMPROMISE, AND SACRIFICE FOR THE GOOD OF THE TEAM

Individuals can influence history, but only groups make history happen. Teamwork is loyalty to a common vision; goodwill towards fellow group members; and cooperation, compromise, and sacrifice for the good of the team; resulting in a united group. Unified groups are strong and aggressive, they remain in power or conquer; while individuals and divided groups are weak and vulnerable, they never attain power or lose it and end up conquered. Teamwork makes us capable of shaping our external world to our advantage, but not working together in teams leaves us very little opportunity for shaping our external world. Working together as a team and staying united is extremely hard work, pride and ambition constantly work to separate us, but teamwork's upside of collective strength far outweighs its costs. Form or join groups sharing our principles, then work collectively towards realizing our group's goals. Never put our individual and subgroup wants above our group's needs, and don't allow small differences to fragment our group; compromise on minor issues to stay strongly united around our group's vision.

SELF-WORTH

ADOPT A POSITIVE SELF-IMAGE AND AVOID A NEGATIVE ONE

How we perceive ourselves significantly affects our capabilities and actions. Self-worth is loving and respecting ourselves and being happy and satisfied with who we are. True self-worth comes from ourselves and our own perceptions and judgements, and never comes from the perceptions and judgments of others. Self-worth gives us a positive self-image and protects us from insecurity, inferiority complexes, low self-esteem, and fear of what others might think or say. With self-worth, we can pursue our hopes, dreams, and aspirations confidently; but without self-worth, a negative self-image prevents us from doing many things we want. Since self-perception is unavoidable, it only makes sense we develop a positive self-image and avoid, at all costs, a negative self-image. Develop self-worth by living consistently with our principles; emphasizing our positives; and fixing, de-emphasizing, or forgiving our shortcomings. Don't be impressed by, in awe of, or feel inferior to anyone because everyone has flaws, personal problems, and skeletons in the closet causing them embarrassment, guilt, and shame: why be impressed by, in awe of, or feel inferior to someone like this? Adopt the motto "No one's better than me, and I'm not better than anyone" for maintaining a positive self-image and avoiding arrogance, then go after what we want confidently.

TOUGHNESS

EMBRACE, ENDURE, AND OVERCOME ALL OBSTACLES

Only the physically and mentally tough survive and thrive. Physical toughness is embracing, enduring, and overcoming exhaustion, hardship, and danger for survival and success. Physically tough people embrace, endure, and overcome heat, cold, filth, hunger, thirst, exhaustion, and danger to attain needs and wants. Physical toughness allows us to overcome difficult situations; while being soft makes us avoid, quit, and submit when faced with difficult situations. Love of easy living and luxury is ok (I guess), but when it makes us soft then the love of easy living and luxury is poison. Be physically tough by getting our hands dirty, sweating, and bleeding to attain our needs and don't allow the fear or dislike of heat, cold, filth, hunger, thirst, exhaustion, and danger stop us from going after what we want.

Mental toughness is neutralizing, enduring, and overcoming abuse, stress, and hardship while maintaining sound mental health. Mentally tough people neutralize, endure, and overcome insults, threats, bullying, humiliation, failure, trauma, torture, and tragedy without succumbing to mental disorders. When we're mentally tough, we can cope with and overcome all difficult situations; but when we're not mentally tough, we're extremely vulnerable to mental disorders that negatively affect our health. All of us will experience (to various degrees) insults, threats, bullying, humiliation, failure, trauma, torture, and tragedy; only mental toughness helps us overcome them all. Mental toughness requires preparation, commitment, and hope. Mentally neutralize abuse, stress, and hardship by expecting them; people will abuse us, life's stresses never end, and hardships are guaranteed; mentally prepare for them beforehand and then mentally accept and deal with their consequences afterward: no surprise, shock, or self-pity. Mentally endure abuse, stress, and hardship by committing to mentally endure all situations; our minds can endure anything when we make simple commitments like "I will endure this abuse," "I will endure this stress," and "I will endure this hardship." Mentally overcome abuse, stress, and hardship by believing and hoping in a better and brighter future for ourselves, our family, our descendants, or our tribe; see it, feel it, taste it, and desire it badly; this hope will drive our ability to overcome all adversities.

A HUMAN'S GUIDE FOR EVERYDAY LIFE

EXPECTATIONS

ASPIRE FOR WHAT'S NATURAL, SIMPLE, AND DOABLE

Our expectations, for ourselves, others, and situations, shape how we perceive our world. Depending on our expectations, the exact same situation can make us content and happy or disappointed and miserable. Proper expectations are natural, simple, and realistic; reflect our goals and aspirations only; and emphasize needs over wants, doable over fantasy, complete human beings over body parts, and whole situations over single events. When we have proper expectations, we're easily made happy, satisfied, and content; but when we have unrealistic expectations, we're almost never happy, satisfied, or content. Unrealistic expectations make us obsessively compare our weaknesses with others' strengths, leaving us always wanting better, always wanting more, and always wanting it right now: under these circumstances, no one can ever be happy, satisfied, or content. Adopt proper expectations by comparing ourselves, our possessions, and our situations with our goals and aspirations only; avoid comparisons with other people, their possessions, their situations, and their expectations; and focus on acquiring necessities and accomplishing doable goals.

DISCIPLINE

DO WHAT BENEFITS YOU, EVEN WHEN YOU DON'T WANT TO; AND DON'T DO WHAT HARMS YOU, EVEN WHEN YOU WANT TO

Without discipline, sooner or later, we will go astray. Discipline is doing what's good for us, even when we don't want to; and not doing what's bad for us, even when we want to. With discipline, we can wake up early in the morning; eat healthy; exercise; learn and work; be punctual; fulfill promises and obligations; be honest, faithful, and trustworthy; control our emotions; ignore evil desires and impulses; and abstain from harming ourselves. When we live disciplined lives, we can act consistently with our principles; complete tasks and projects excellently; and achieve our goals; but when we live undisciplined lives, we end up slaves to bad habits, evil desires, and wild emotions; sloppy and lazy; unable to complete tasks and projects excellently;

and incapable of achieving our goals. We can't control what we like, crave, or desire, but we can control what we do; discipline empowers us to choose what we do and what we don't do. Do actions and adopt routines that are advantageous and abstain from actions and routines that are disadvantageous (see Chapter 4 *Raising and Razing Habits*).

EFFORT

BE PREPARED, PRECISE, AND PERSISTENT

Success requires excellence, and excellence is achieved only through our sincerely best effort, which is being prepared, precise, and persistent. Prepared means all relevant information is acquired, all necessary skills and knowledge are learned, and all impending actions are rehearsed and mastered; precise means fulfilling requirements and expectations by confirming each step's correctness through double-checking, reading twice, and using checklists; and persistent means overcoming barriers, setbacks, and missteps to complete our task, project, or goal. Giving our sincerely best effort optimizes outcomes and assures us the best destiny possible; while not giving our sincerely best effort usually results in failure or sloppy, subpar outcomes. Giving our sincerely best effort doesn't guarantee success, but it does guarantee us the highest level of success possible. Always give our sincerely best effort by being prepared, precise, and persistent in all we do.

DESTINY

GIVE YOUR SINCERELY BEST EFFORT, THEN ACCEPT OUTCOMES AS DESTINY

We have total control over our effort, but we don't have total control over outcomes; ultimately, outcomes lie in the hands of destiny. Many smart, energetic, and capable people who give their sincerely best effort their entire lives never achieve their goals; while sometimes mildly talented, half-sloppy, half-lazy people do achieve their goals. Believing effort is entirely within our control, but outcomes are not, motivates us to pursue favorable outcomes while preparing us mentally for unfavorable ones; but believing we have total control over outcomes leaves us mentally unprepared to deal with unfavorable results, exposing us to heartbreak, depression, and despair.

Never use destiny as an excuse for sloppiness and laziness because the general rule applies that excellent effort results in excellent outcomes and sloppy effort results in sloppy outcomes, just remember excellent effort doesn't guarantee excellent outcomes. Always give our sincerely best effort and then accept outcomes, whether good or bad, as destiny.

FORGIVENESS

FORGIVE YOURSELF, NO MATTER WHAT

Forgiving others is fine, but the best forgiveness is self-forgiveness. Self-forgiveness is pardoning our mistakes, failures, and unfulfilled aspirations; it's very important because many health problems stem from a lack of self-forgiveness. No matter how bad our mistake, big our failure, or disastrous the outcome, we must forgive ourselves wholeheartedly and move on. Self-forgiveness provides us with absolution, redemption, and renewed hope for the future; while not forgiving ourselves leaves us guilt-ridden, stuck dwelling on the past, and extremely vulnerable to stress-related health problems. Despite being very important for our mental and physical health, and though it should come naturally, self-forgiveness is one of the most difficult habits to develop; for some reason, we love beating ourselves up over the past. After giving our sincerely best effort, forgive ourselves of everything: all our mistakes, failures, and unfulfilled aspirations, no matter how disastrous or tragic the outcome; and move on with renewed hope, no guilt, and no regrets.

HOPE

BE OPTIMISTIC AND NEVER LOSE HOPE

To keep going, we need hope a better and brighter future is coming soon. Hope is expecting negative patterns and trends to stop and become positive, and positive patterns and trends to continue and improve. Belief and hope in a better and brighter future generate the energy we need to endure and overcome hardships, difficulties, and challenges. When we're hopeful, we're optimistic, mentally tough, and perseverant; but when we lose hope, we're pessimistic, mentally fragile, and quick to quit. Only belief and hope in a better and brighter future create the "never give up" spirit shared by all conquerors, champions, and winners. Keep believing and hoping a better and brighter future is possible, if not for us, then for our family, descendants, or tribe; see it, feel it, taste it, and desire it badly. This desire will drive our ability to endure and overcome all obstacles, no matter what the current circumstances may be.

PREEMINENT PROVERBS FOR EVERYDAY LIFE

THOSE WHO MAKE THE RULES WIN

- When we set the rules, all is possible, and our advantage is guaranteed.

DON'T BE A NAIVE SUCKER

- Many people care only about themselves and will do anything to get what they want; never let anyone use, abuse, bully, humiliate, trick, fool, cheat, con, or hustle us; if they wouldn't do it for us, then we don't do it for them; and extreme skepticism, rigorous investigation, concrete evidence, and clear understanding all come before our belief.

MAKE PEOPLE FEEL HOW YOU WANT THEM TO FEEL

- To get what we want, give the right message, to the right people, at the right time.

IF YOU WANT IT, THEN GO GET IT

- No effort equals no results; don't sit around waiting, hoping, and wishing for things to happen, make things happen.

THINK LIKE THE CONQUEROR

- Be confident, optimistic, and bold; avoid inferiority complexes, insecurities, and self-doubt; feel dominant and pursue dominance; and never feel or think like a victim.

WEALTH COMES FROM RELATIONSHIPS

- Meaningful relationships, with the right people, are more fruitful than intelligence, talent, and drive.

LIFE IS ABOUT ADJUSTMENTS

- Life's situations are constantly changing, expect and embrace change because it's unavoidable.

CONFIRM EVERYTHING

- Make sure our work, information, and understanding are correct by double-checking, rereading, using checklists, cross-checking, and scrutinizing sources.

REMOVE BARRIERS

- Barriers create trouble, friction, and hassle, which block us from getting what we want and doing what we must.

AVOID NEGATIVE INFLUENCES

- Positively influence, be positively influenced, or cut relations, because everyone we associate with and everything we watch, listen to, and read affects our thoughts, beliefs, and actions.

TODAY IS NOT THE SAME AS YESTERDAY, TOMORROW IS NOT THE SAME AS TODAY

- Patterns and trends, whether positive, negative, well-established, or long-lasting, are not guaranteed to continue; every day is filled with completely new possibilities, negative patterns and trends can be changed and positive patterns and trends must be maintained with maximum effort, or they could end.

THERE IS A SOLUTION FOR EVERY PROBLEM

- If we think or try hard enough, and we're creative, we will find a way to fix our situation.

LIVE BRAVE, DIE BRAVE

- Overcome our fear and do what we must, embrace conflict because conflict that can't be avoided shouldn't be, and be willing to sacrifice our lives for our principles, family, and tribe: death is certain, so why fear it?

TRUISM TRIPLETS FOR EVERYDAY LIFE

GRAB ATTENTION, THEN CREATE BELIEF, THEN FULFILL PROMISES

- Get what we want ethically by making our message known, convincing people its benefits are real, and delivering promised value.

- Con artists grab attention, then create belief, then extract as much as possible, then cut relations; never do this.

INSULT WORSE THAN YOU WERE INSULTED, HIT HARDER THAN YOU WERE HIT, AND BE TOUGH BECAUSE LIFE IS TOUGH

- Retaliate when wronged because predators target those who don't fight back.

- Expect and be prepared for life's adversities, challenges, and hardships, because they'll be with us from the cradle to the grave, and especially be ready for people trying to put us down to build themselves up: no shock, no sadness, and no tears.

POSITIVE IS USUALLY BETTER THAN NEGATIVE, SIMPLE IS USUALLY BETTER THAN COMPLEX, AND DOABLE IS ALWAYS BETTER THAN FANTASY

- View situations, solve problems, and express ourselves in ways that accomplish our goals, make us feel good, and leave others feeling good about themselves and us.

- Don't make things difficult when they don't need to be.

- Work towards achieving what's possible instead of dreaming of perfect scenarios that are impossible.

SHARE ONLY WHAT NEEDS TO BE KNOWN, DON'T BE AFRAID TO SAY "NO," AND NEVER TRY PLEASING PEOPLE YOU CAN'T

- Jealously guard our secrets, personal information, and plans because the only way to guarantee they won't be used against us is by making sure no one knows them.

- Don't do something just because someone tells us to or because everyone else is, and don't take something just because it's easy or free; ignore, refuse, or reject requests, offers, or orders we don't want to do, make us uncomfortable, we neither need nor want, and are not to our advantage.

- Realize some people will never be satisfied with us, no matter what we do.

THE MOUNTAIN IS CLIMBED ONE STEP AT A TIME, EVERYTHING IS HARD THE FIRST TIME, AND YOU CAN'T WIN IF YOU'RE AFRAID TO LOSE

- Small, steady accomplishments accumulate into major results.

- Beginnings are almost always filled with discomfort, hardship, and failure: don't give up.

- Fear of loss and failure impedes the boldness, clear thinking, and calculated risk-taking necessary for success: don't be afraid of losing or failing, be afraid of not trying.

TREAT PEOPLE HOW YOU WANT TO BE TREATED, NEVER SAY WHAT YOU REALLY DON'T MEAN, AND DON'T GIVE PROBLEMS AND HARDSHIPS—GIVE SOLUTIONS

- Treat everyone with dignity and respect; never embarrass people or make them feel uncomfortable; no bullying; don't crush others' dreams; keep people's secrets secret; stay away from their wealth, family members, and love interests; don't force anyone to do what they don't want to, even if we think it's good for them; apologize when wrong; and reward kindness with gratitude.

- Never make a promise we can't keep, make a threat we're unwilling to carry out, or hurt loved ones with careless insults.

- Make people's lives better and easier: no criticism, complaints, or prohibitions without solutions.

LEARN FROM THE PAST, LIVE IN THE PRESENT, PLAN FOR THE FUTURE

- Don't dwell on what has already happened, and don't worry too much about what hasn't happened yet; focus our resources (time, energy, money) on what's going on right now because only today can we fix or atone for our past and only today can we positively shape our future.

DO IT YOURSELF IF YOU CAN, ASK FOR HELP IF YOU CAN'T, AND DON'T ASK FOR WHAT CAN'T BE GIVEN

- Asking for help when we could do something ourselves is shameful, and not asking for help when we truly need it is also shameful: we all need each other's help for survival and success.

- Don't insist on borrowing $1,000 if our friend has only $500, don't expect our son to carry 200 pounds if he can carry only 100 pounds, and don't demand help in the morning if our cousin can help only in the evening: be reasonable in our requests.

SPEND WITHIN YOUR MEANS, DON'T WASTE RESOURCES, AND IT'S NOT YOURS UNTIL IT'S IN YOUR HANDS

- Aspire for better while living how we can afford to live today.

- Enjoy meals, but don't overindulge; buy only what we'll use, and never to show-off.

- Don't consider something ours until we fully own and control it.

DON'T ASK A QUESTION IF YOU'RE AFRAID OF THE ANSWER, LEARN LESSONS THE FIRST TIME, AND BEWARE—ANYTHING COULD BE ANYWHERE

- Don't investigate if we're unwilling or unable to deal with the consequences.

- Avoid making the same mistakes over, and over, and over again.

- Always be on the lookout for potential dangers, both small and great; road hazards, thieves, murderers, rapists, and child molesters could be anywhere or anyone.

NEVER ASK FOR YOUR GIFTS BACK, KNOCK BEFORE OPENING DOORS, AND DON'T BLOCK PATHS

- Don't use our gifts as weapons of manipulation and spite because gifts already given no longer belong to us.

- Save ourselves from seeing what we shouldn't.

- Prevent ourselves from frustrating others unnecessarily.

GIVE FULL SERVICE, EXCELLENCE IS JUST A LITTLE EXTRA EFFORT AWAY, AND FINISH THE RACE

- When we choose to do something for someone, do it excellently, with a smile, and leave them happy and satisfied.

- The distance between sloppiness and excellence (maybe 10% extra effort) is far less than the distance between zero effort and sloppiness.

- Don't quit giving our sincerely best effort until we've completed our task, project, or goal: a final burst of energy, enthusiasm, and effort at the end often leads to success.

2
A HUMAN'S GUIDE TO RICHES

Those who consume interest will not stand except as one driven mad by Satan's touch; that's because they say trading is like loaning money at interest, but Allah permits trading and forbids loaning money at interest. Whoever receives their Lord's admonition and stops (consuming interest) may keep what has already passed, and their affair rests with Allah, but whoever returns (to consuming interest) they are the companions of Hell, they will live there forever.

—The Qur'an 2:275 (translation)

WIN-WIN EXCHANGES

With every business transaction, we choose between good and bad business. Good business is honest, transparent, and consensual exchanges based on mutual benefit. When both we and those we're doing business with benefit from an exchange, we both feel satisfied and want to do business with each other again. Bad business is applying warfare rules to business, pushing one-sided, "I win, you lose" exchanges. In war, we ethically lie and cheat (war is deception), steal (raid and plunder), and kill (diminish enemy's strength), but warfare rules don't apply to business because war and business aren't the same. People conducting business using warfare rules aren't good businessmen, they're con artists, thieves, and murderers. When we conduct business pursuing mutually beneficial exchanges, people want to do business with us over and over again and our reputation as good people to do business with spreads; but when we conduct business pushing one-sided, "I win, you lose" exchanges, no one wants to do business with us twice and our reputation as people not to do business with spreads. Be aware, mutually beneficial doesn't necessarily mean equally beneficial: both buyer and seller beware. Conduct business in a way that benefits us, makes people want to do business with us again, spreads our reputation as good people to do business with, and doesn't make us go to prison or burn in Hell.

ARTFUL NEGOTIATIONS

A product, service, or labor is worth what sellers and buyers agree to sell and buy it for; get good deals and avoid being ripped off with artful negotiations. Artful negotiations are buying and selling goods, services, and labor at the price point (sale or purchase price) we want by knowing market prices, committing to our desired price point, using human psychology to our advantage, and walking away from bad deals. Before negotiations begin, know the current market price, set our desired price point, and begin negotiations with our price point a well-kept secret. When selling or buying in a standard free market environment (with multiple sellers and buyers and alternative goods, services, and labor), start negotiations with an asking price (when selling) higher than our price point or an offer (when buying) lower than our price point; this makes our real price point, which comes later, more attractive. Make sure our initial high asking price or low offer isn't so high or low it causes those we're negotiating with to end negotiations because they feel we're tricking, cheating, or hustling them. Also, beware of the initial high asking price or low offer coming from those we're negotiating with, never use it for comparison, only use our price point for comparison. If, after a few rounds of trading asking prices and offers we haven't come to an agreement at our desired price point, test the other side's commitment to their asking price or offer by threatening to walk away from the deal; for our test to be effective, our threat must be believable. When selling in an auction-style environment (one seller of one good, service, or labor and multiple potential buyers), make potential buyers bid against each other openly, allowing their desire to win drive up our sale price. The highest offer isn't necessarily the best; other factors for choosing the winning bid are guarantees of quality craftsmanship and service, hassle-free payment processes, discounts, and future business. When buying in an auction-style environment, start with our real price point and sweeten the offer with guarantees of quality craftsmanship and service, hassle-free payment processes, discounts, and future business. Whether selling or buying, walk away from bad deals and never sell below or buy above our price point, except when absolutely necessary.

A HUMAN'S GUIDE TO RICHES

MAKING MONEY

Whether we're selling products, services, or labor, the process is the same; making money is a loop of identifying potential consumers, advertising to them, completing sales, and delivering promised value. First, identify potential customers or employers and make them aware of what we're offering. Next, make our prospective customer or employer feel he needs or wants our product, service, or labor; convince him what we're offering is more valuable than his money and is a better solution than his alternatives. Now, close the deal by making the purchase of our product, service, or labor friction and hassle-free. Finally, leave our customer or employer happy and satisfied by delivering promised value. Remember, our product, service, or labor is worth exactly what we can convince a buyer or employer to pay for it: no more, no less.

GROWING WEALTH

No matter what our current financial situation is, we can improve it. Growing wealth is a simple formula of increasing income, decreasing spending, acquiring assets, and avoiding liabilities. Increase income by making more money per hour worked or working more hours, or by making more money per sale or making more sales. Decrease spending by reducing or eliminating the purchase of non-essentials (wants), paying less for purchases through discounts (coupons and sales) or choosing cheaper alternatives (switching to Ketchup X or Mustard Y because it's cheaper than our usual brand of ketchup), and increasing efficiency in the use of purchases (making a tube of toothpaste last ten days instead of seven). Use as much of our wealth as possible to acquire assets (possessions continuously increasing in value, and their increase in value is greater than their costs) and avoid liabilities (possessions continuously decreasing in value, or their costs are greater than their increase in value). No matter how alluring, prestigious, or desirable they may be, stay away from liabilities; they keep poor people poor, and keep middle class people stuck in the middle class or make them poor, and make rich people middle class or poor. Also, be aware today's asset can become tomorrow's liability; once we're positive an asset has become a liability, dump it.

A HUMAN'S GUIDE FOR EVERYDAY LIFE

BUILDING BUSINESSES

Great businesses focus on pleasing their customers by giving them what they want, when and how they want it. Fulfill needs (life's necessities), satisfy wants (life's delights), or remove hassle (life's drudgeries). Make our customers feel healthier (mentally, physically, spiritually), wealthier (money and asset growth), wiser (knowledge and know-how), safer (secure from danger), more loved (sweethearts, family, friends), more prestigious (status and power), or more entertained (pleasure and excitement). Avoid bad customers (customers purchasing very little despite requiring high levels of attention, time, and energy) by eliminating them without hurting and disrespecting them, and nurture relationships with good customers (customers purchasing much, or purchasing little while requiring low levels of attention, time, and energy) by making them feel appreciated and important.

FINDING EMPLOYMENT

Our jobs brighten or darken our lives, choose the positive employment path and avoid the negative. Begin by picking an industry compatible with our desired lifestyle, make sure we're satisfied with its potential salary, then get the credentials necessary for working in it (certifications, degrees, work experience). Specializing in high-demand skills results in more employment opportunities and higher salaries; whereas, not having in-demand specialized skills leaves us drowning in competition and relying on luck for attractive employment opportunities: prepare properly for our employment future. Next, use our network of family, friends, colleagues, and acquaintances to help us find employment. An employer knowing us, or knowing someone who knows us, is more likely to hire us than an employer to whom we're complete strangers. Get hired by convincing our potential employer we'll make him money and stay employed by continuously showing our employer we're making him money; make him feel we're very valuable and worth much more than he's paying us. Keep our skillset up to date because everyone's replaceable; the moment we're no longer viewed as an asset, we'll be let go.

NETWORKING

It's always easier dealing with people we know or a "friend of a friend"; and meaningful relationships with the right people are more likely to make us rich than intelligence, talent, and drive; so, take networking seriously. Build a large and diverse network composed of family, friends, colleagues, and acquaintances. From our network, develop connections based on mutual benefit, shared interests, and common goals. Turn to our network when needing products, services, and labor, and let everyone in our network know the products, services, and labor we're offering. Ask for help only when we truly need it, help at least as much as we're helped, and never satisfy unreasonable requests or help people with what they can easily do themselves. Access to help is a priceless asset: use it wisely and don't abuse it.

BILLIONAIRE BONANZAS

Becoming and staying among the world's wealthiest demands extraordinary measures, build our billionaire bonanza by (legally) creating or pinpointing loopholes, weaknesses, or malfunctions, then capitalizing on them with extreme control and concentration. Control markets (not the best choice, but the only choice), control resources (water, mineral, energy), control networks (computer and internet platforms, railroad tracks and air and sea ports, banking and credit), control innovation (turn great ideas into cash cows), control media (make people believe what we want them to believe), control force (security, police, military), and control laws (spin local, national, and international laws into gold); concentrate assets (use size for crushing competitors and squeezing sweet deals out of suppliers, big money beats little money), concentrate talent (those knowing how to make money make even more money together), concentrate risk (give all risk to others, privatize gains and socialize losses, be too big to fail, and use other people's money to make money—for us), and concentrate political power (taxes and tribute, it's great being king).

A HUMAN'S GUIDE FOR EVERYDAY LIFE

WEALTHY SOCIETIES

Governments don't know how to create wealth for their citizens, they know only how to extract it from them; it's individuals who know best how to create wealth for themselves; this is why wealthy societies promote economic freedom and allow their citizens to make their own economic decisions. In wealthy societies, citizens choose their occupations and change them at will; live where they want and can move anytime; buy and sell desired products, services, and labor at prices buyers and sellers agree upon; and spend their money as they wish. When citizens are economically free, society enjoys increased motivation; superior customer service; high quality products, services, and labor; more choice; lower prices; advances in technology; and economic growth. When governments direct the economy, citizens suffer reduced motivation; bad customer service; poor quality products, services, and labor; less choice; high prices; and stagnated innovation; even with good intentions like citizens' safety, protecting jobs, economic equality, and economic growth, governments directing the economy depresses economic growth and causes economic meltdowns: over the past hundred years alone, millions upon millions have starved to death due to governments misdirecting their economies. Also, wealthy societies don't punish their rich citizens with punitive taxes meant to equalize economic status because this makes society poorer, not more equal. We have different levels of ability, drive, and determination, resulting in some outshining others: this is why wealth concentrates at the top. Just as attempting to equalize strength, speed, and intelligence would be detrimental to society, equalizing economic achievement is similarly detrimental. Unfortunately, just as there will always be some having less strength, speed, and intelligence, there will always be some having less wealth; as long as all citizens have basic food, clothing, shelter, and lifelong opportunities to improve, develop, and grow, all citizens must be free to chase their economic dreams and make as much (legal) money as they can: this is the closest we'll ever come to a fair economic system for all.

3
CHARISMATIC INFLUENCE

Invite to the way of your Lord with wisdom and beautiful exhortations and argue with them in the best way: certainly, your Lord knows best who has strayed from His path and who is guided.

—The Qur'an 16:125 (translation)

CHARISMATIC MAGNETISM

We're attracted to confidence; therefore, making people feel we're confident attracts them to us. Charismatic magnetism is a set of internal attitudes and external behaviors sending subconscious messages of confidence and self-assuredness to our external world. Most of our judgments about others, especially initially, are made by subconsciously interpreting subtle cues projected by others. We tend to accept what others project; so, when we transmit charismatic magnetism to those around us, we'll generally be believed. Projecting charismatic magnetism leads to many people liking us and wanting us to like them, making influencing and persuading them much easier; while not projecting charismatic magnetism results in less people liking us and caring what we think about them, weaker ability to influence and persuade, and a harder time getting what we want. Whether we naturally have "it" or not, charismatic magnetism is a skill that can be learned or improved upon by anyone. Learn and implement the three elements of charismatic magnetism—internal peace, alpha body language, and connective interactions—and make projecting confidence and self-assuredness our habit.

INTERNAL PEACE

Charismatic magnetism begins with internal peace, the source of our confidence and self-assuredness. Internal peace is a loop of living consistently with our principles, self-worth, mental toughness, proper expectations, giving our sincerely best effort, belief in destiny, self-forgiveness, and hope in a better and brighter future (see Chapter 1). Living consistently with our principles establishes and confirms our identity, purpose, and meaning; self-worth gives us the self-love and self-respect we so desperately need; mental toughness provides us the mental strength to cope with all difficulties; proper expectations allow us to be satisfied with natural and realistic conditions and situations; giving our sincerely best effort assures us the best destiny possible; belief in destiny allows us to accept and deal with non-optimal outcomes; self-forgiveness helps us overcome our mistakes, failures, and unfulfilled aspirations; and hope in a better and brighter future fuels our perseverant, "never give up" spirit. When we have internal peace, we're confident and self-assured; but when we don't have internal peace, we can never genuinely be confident and self-assured. Though it's true internal peace can be "faked" through visualization techniques, it's to our advantage to truly be confident and self-assured. Establish and maintain the loop of internal peace, then project our confidence and self-assuredness to our external world with alpha body language and connective interactions.

ALPHA BODY LANGUAGE

Alpha body language is a set of non-verbal cues sending subconscious messages of confidence and self-assuredness to those around us. Applying some of these non-verbal cues will immediately feel comfortable, while others may seem awkward at first; with practice, all alpha body language can feel as natural as any of our other habits. Making alpha body language our habit enables us to consistently project confidence and self-assuredness, while not making alpha body language our habit leaves us not knowing what subconscious messages we're projecting. Alpha body language has been taught to monarchs in training for millennia and is the source of their appearing "regal." Sit, stand, and walk like the king/queen: head up, back straight, shoulders back, chest out, and expand; embrace stillness and silence; be relaxed, calm, and comfortable; inhale and exhale through our nose; look people directly in the eyes; and smile. Abstain from slouching, fidgeting, stress and anxiety filled exhales from our mouth, and avoiding eye contact. For activating or resetting alpha body language, take a deep breath, close our eyes for a second, then think "expand and smile." Always use alpha body language for projecting confidence and self-assuredness, especially during connective interactions.

CONNECTIVE INTERACTIONS

During interactions, we love feeling accepted, paid attention to, liked, and respected; connective interactions enable us to listen and speak with people in a way that leaves them feeling how we all love feeling. When we practice connective interactions, we make people feel good, about themselves and us; but when we don't practice connective interactions, there's an increased chance of leaving people feeling disappointed, disrespected, and rejected. The key to connective interactions is goodwill towards all; want good for everyone because others having good doesn't take away anything from us. Be mentally present during all interactions by giving our full attention, don't look at or think about anything but the people we're interacting with. Radiate warmth by showing we care; be aware of, and concerned with, people's feelings and emotions; make them feel their happiness makes us happy, their sadness makes us sad, and we genuinely want to help them. Share their emotions; laugh with them, cry with them, contemplate and explore possibilities with them. During greetings and departures, give warm handshakes while maintaining eye contact and smiling. Accept praise with eye contact, a friendly smile, and a warm "thank you." Avoid repelling with bad hygiene; disgusting habits; or an excessive, undignified eagerness to please. Also, most people assume all actions and reactions around them are about them, don't let our physical or mental discomforts be misinterpreted. If we're not feeling the emotions needed for a positive interaction, take a deep breath, close our eyes for a second, then think of our desired emotion (friendship, admiration, compassion). While listening, demonstrate we're engaged with a single nod, "yes," or "ah-ha" every few sentences. Allow people to complete their thoughts before speaking and never interrupt, even to praise. If we become distracted, take a deep breath, close our eyes for a moment, then think "connect." Pause two seconds and fully absorb what was said before replying; speak audibly, clearly, and not too fast; lower intonation at the end of statements; raise intonation at the end of questions; avoid making sounds such as "ah," "um," etc. and pause briefly between sentences to breathe. Paint verbal pictures and images that resonate, make our messages memorable using all five senses, and focus on making people feel how we want them to feel. Once we've made a connection, people are open to our persuasive influence.

A HUMAN'S GUIDE FOR EVERYDAY LIFE
PERSUASIVE INFLUENCE

Persuasive influence is making people want to do what we want them to do, when and how we want them to do it. Persuasive influence pursues consensual, mutually beneficial, win-win outcomes. Any persuasion or influence pushing one-sided, "I win, you lose" outcomes is not persuasive influence; it's manipulation, exploitation, conning, and hustling. When we practice persuasive influence, everyone wins and everyone ends up happy and satisfied; but when we pursue one-sided outcomes through manipulation, exploitation, conning, and hustling, we unjustly harm people and become terrible, loathsome, disgusting human beings. Be aware mutually beneficial doesn't necessarily mean equally beneficial; persuasion which both parties benefit from, and doesn't contain deception, is persuasive influence. Use persuasive influence to make people want to do what we want them to do, when and how we want them to do it.

Persuasive influence begins with making people want to do what we want them to do, our desired action, by making them feel our desired action benefits them. Do this by appealing to both their conscious and subconscious pursuit of perceived advantage, convince them the benefit of doing our desired action is real, and make them want it badly. When we make people feel doing our desired action benefits them, getting them to take action is easy; but when we don't make people feel doing our desired action benefits them, getting them to take action is very difficult. The pursuit of perceived advantage manifests itself through conscious decisions (people contemplating, debating, and then choosing to do our desired action) and subconscious pressures (cravings, desires, and impulses pushing people towards doing our desired action). Present people with a problem or opportunity, make them feel solving it or capitalizing on it will benefit them, then give them the solution which solves the problem or enables them to capitalize on the opportunity: our desired action. The following fifteen influence aids utilize people's conscious and subconscious pursuit of perceived advantage to get them listening to our message of problems or opportunities, feeling it benefits them, and wanting to do our desired action:

1. We're emotional beings, so construct emotional messages using images and stories people relate to, supported by facts, that introduce them to our message, convince them it's beneficial, and make them want to do our desired action.

2. We favor our tribesmen and prefer interacting and doing business with them, but generally dislike and distrust outsiders (foreigners and out-group members); make people feel we're part of their tribe, one of them, and on their side (similar origins, experiences, beliefs, and hobbies) so they'll be open to listening to our message, feeling it benefits them, and doing our desired action.

3. We love praise and desire to please and reward those who praise us; sincerely and specifically compliment people and what they value so they'll want to please and reward us by listening to our message, feeling it benefits them, and doing our desired action. Praise with compliments ("Do you work out? You look really fit," "Your team looks like they're going all the way this year," "You did a great job on that project"), special recognitions ("We usually don't do this, but we're going to do it for you"), and written acknowledgments (certificates of achievement, employee of the month, thank you letters).

4. When others do something for us, we feel a strong need to reciprocate; do, give, or say something people consider valuable ("valuable" means useful, not necessarily expensive) so they'll feel they must repay us by listening to our message, feeling it benefits them, and doing our desired action. Give our gift before requesting our desired action to ensure our gift isn't perceived to be a bribe.

5. We associate emotions with people, places, objects, and sensations; if we can link positive emotions with us and our desired action, people will want to listen to us, believe us, and do our desired action. Create a positive emotional experience for people and link the positive emotions with us and our desired action (treat them to a delicious meal, take them to a sporting event, accompany them for an enjoyable walk in the park) or cause people to relive the emotions of a previous positive experience and link these positive emotions with us and our desired action (give them their favorite food, take them to their favorite place, talk about their most cherished memories).

6. We need to act consistently with our principles and become very uncomfortable when we don't; show people their actions are inconsistent with their principles and make them feel our desired action is the solution restoring consistency.

7. We desire fairness; make people feel they're not getting their fair share or are being treated unfairly, then convince them our desired action restores fairness.

8. We use others' behavior to determine what is proper and improper behavior; convince people our desired action is either the current social norm (standard) or becoming the new social norm (hottest new trend) so they'll want to do it.

9. We obey authority, experts, and those we admire; make people feel we have legitimate authority, are genuine experts, or deserve admiration, and they'll listen to our message, believe it, and want to do our desired action.

10. We're influenced by others' expectations; make our expectations known, that people will do our desired action, through verbal and non-verbal messages ("What time will I pick you up?"; "Are you paying with cash or credit?"; present a contract that needs only signing).

11. Small agreements and small involvement lead to big agreements and big involvement; start with a small agreement or small request for involvement and build from there, one "yes" opens the door to many. Once we've established ourselves as someone people say "yes" to, compliance is possible in all areas.

12. We use comparison to help make judgements and decisions, so make our desired action appear more attractive by contrasting it with a less attractive alternative:

    - Offer a lesser value or undesirable choice followed by our greater value or more desirable choice, our desired action, for the exact same price (time, energy, money, consequences).

    - When selling, start with a high asking price followed by our real (lower) asking price (our desired action).

    - When buying, start with a low offer followed by our real (higher) offer (our desired action).

- Turn one large payment into multiple smaller payments (A $300 fee becomes "Three easy payments of $100," $1,000 a year becomes "Less than $84 a month," Thirty hours a month becomes "Only one hour a day").

13. We hate losing what we believe belongs to us (our current possessions and freedom to add new possessions); threatening to take away the opportunity to do our desired action makes people want to do our desired action now. Set deadlines ("Offer ends tomorrow"), limit space ("Only two seats left"), limit numbers ("Just one left in stock"), and restrict access ("Exclusively for first ten customers").

14. Desire for current and future benefits overwhelms our loyalty to the source of past benefits; keep people loyal by assuring them our desired action continues providing accustomed benefits and win people over by convincing them our desired action is the best source of benefits from this point forward.

15. We're extremely attracted to optimism and hope, give the hopeless hope in a better and brighter future and they'll do anything to get it; fill people with belief and hope that our desired action provides them a better and brighter future and they'll definitely want to do it.

After making people want to do our desired action, instruct them when and how to do it. Make our instructions clear (necessary who, what, where, when, how, and why explained), specific (steps A-Z defined), and doable (achievable, simple, and hassle-free). Making our instructions clear, specific, and doable is the best way to ensure our desired action is completed correctly; while not making our instructions clear, specific, and doable usually results in our desired action not being completed correctly. It doesn't benefit anyone if we make people want to do our desired action, but then they don't do it or don't complete it correctly. Clearly and specifically instruct people how to complete our desired action and make completing it as simple and hassle-free as possible. Leave those we're influencing and persuading happy and satisfied by making them feel their compliance is consensual (give them a few options, two best, for completing our desired action: "Do you want to meet today or tomorrow?"; "Are you joining our one-month or three-month program?"; "Do you want your initiation ceremony to be public or private?") and by ensuring our desired action delivers on its promised benefits.

4
LEARNING EFFICIENCY HABITS

In the messenger of Allah (the prophet Muhammad), you definitely have an excellent role model for whoever's hopes are in Allah and the last day and remembers Allah much.

—The Qur'an 33:21 (translation)

EFFECTIVE EFFICIENCY

Maximizing benefits and minimizing costs is the essence of advantage. Effective efficiency is doing the tasks and projects which move us closest to achieving our goals while spending the least amount of time, energy, and money completing them. Do this by limiting tasks and projects to only the most important and resources spent to the absolute minimum. When we practice effective efficiency, we accomplish what truly matters without wasting resources; and when we don't practice effective efficiency, we may accomplish some of our goals, but we'll fall short of our full potential and waste precious resources. We all have tasks and projects we work on every day; doesn't it make sense to do what benefits us most and save our limited resources for future achievements? Do only the most beneficial tasks and projects with the least amount of resources by planning, imagining, executing, evaluating, deciding, solving, and systematizing.

PLANNING

Effective efficiency begins with planning. Planning is deciding what to do and in what order, how and when to do it, and who and what are needed to do it. Planning works for simple and complex tasks, small and large projects, and lifetime goals. Start by deciding what we want to accomplish: our end-goal. Clearly and specifically define what successfully completing our end-goal is to confirm it's doable and know it when it's achieved. Next, identify and order all steps necessary for achieving our end-goal, set a time or date for achieving it, and erect milestones with deadlines to ensure we complete our end-goal on time. Plan on appointing the most capable people available for completing each step, clearly and specifically explain our expectations, then empower them to take all necessary actions to meet our expectations. Plan on using only appropriate tools and materials, not the cheapest, because using low quality or inappropriate tools and equipment results in wasted time, energy, and money. Finally, make our plan into a prioritized and scheduled list, then prepare to execute it by imagining success.

IMAGINING

We can achieve only what we believe, and imagining success creates belief. Imagining success is visualizing ourselves successfully completing each step of our plan before execution. Our mind can't easily distinguish reality from fantasy, so when we imagine successfully completing our plan during preparations, our mind will feel we've genuinely done it; and if we've successfully completed something once before, we definitely can do it again. When we imagine successfully completing our plan, we're mentally prepared for success; but when we don't imagine successfully completing our plan, we're not. Imagining success is vital for everything we do—learning, working, training—never neglect it. Before executing our plan, turn it into a mental movie; vividly, specifically, and with emotion, imagine completing each step of our plan precisely until we've visualized completing it successfully; see it, feel it, hear it, smell it, and taste it happening step by step. Finally, imagine feeling satisfaction, pleasure, and joy after successfully completing our plan and praise ourselves for a job well done ("I did a great job, I'm very proud of myself"). After we've imagined successfully executing our plan, it's time to really do it.

EXECUTING

Executing our plan begins by concentrating all our resources towards completing each step on our list precisely, in order, and on schedule. Since beginnings are the hardest part of any endeavor, avoid procrastination by starting the first item on our list immediately. Do each step one at a time because attention (moment to moment focus) takes time to kick in and is never achieved while multitasking. Multitasking is the ultimate focus, attention, and concentration killer, never do it. Make each work session friction and interruption-free:

- Assign everything (keys, wallets, files) a "home" so we don't waste time searching for things when we need them.

- Remove all barriers preventing, discouraging, or slowing down efficiency before work session begins.

- Keep work area clean and organized before, during, and after work session because dirty and messy is inefficient.

- Don't accept phone calls, emails, text messages, and visitors until our work session is finished because stopping and restarting destroys attention and can make a work session cost double or triple its appropriate time.

Confirm (double-check, reread, use checklists) all our work because confirming eliminates most mistakes. Also, don't be distracted by what is supposedly urgent; most beneficial takes priority over urgent but not as beneficial. Delegate all we can to capable people, clearly and specifically explain our expectations, then empower them to take all necessary actions to meet our expectations; and don't give too much work to anyone, neither ourselves nor others, because overworked people produce sloppy results. When dealing with others, deal only with final decision makers (those having the power and authority to say "yes" or "no"), get information only from those who truly know (so we're not confused or misled by incorrect information), and use charismatic influence (see Chapter 3) to get people wanting to do what we want them to do.

EVALUATING

Evaluating our progress is done while we're executing our plan. After every completed step, ask these four questions:

1. Are we moving closer to achieving our goal?

2. Is there something else we can do that moves us closer to achieving our goal faster?

3. Can we execute our plan quicker, easier, or using less resources?

4. Are we completing our work excellently?

Remember, excellently means precisely, as required, and to expectations; excellently doesn't mean perfectly. Avoid chasing perfection because perfection is unattainable; therefore, pursuing it is inefficient and wasteful.

DECIDING

To achieve greatness and avoid catastrophe, we need to make quick and decisive decisions. Quick and decisive decisions are essential at all stages of effective efficiency, they're how we seize opportunity and avert tragedy. Acting slowly or indecisively results in opportunities passing us by and small problems becoming big. When we make quick and decisive decisions, we seize advantage; but when we don't make quick and decisive decisions, advantage slips through our fingers. Never delay due to fear of making the wrong decision because mistakes are overcome much easier than indecision. The following is how we make quick and decisive decisions:

1. Identify our need or want.

2. Contrast our options.

3. Select the most advantageous option.

Also, use decision templates (general rules of conduct decided in advance such as "I do not leave my children alone with men," "I do not donate large amounts of money to strangers," "I do not pay in full until all work is completed") and trust and follow our decision templates over our heart, gut, and instincts.

SOLVING

To be effectively efficient, solve problems directly and indirectly. Directly solve problems by addressing the problem's source and fixing it; gather information (meet the people, visit the places, and see the things involved with the problem), contrast our options, then make quick and decisive decisions. When problems can't be solved directly, solve them indirectly by replacing the unsolvable problem with a solvable one that makes the unsolvable problem go away or become irrelevant; for example, if we want to get rid of the hundredth link in a chain, but can't cut or break it, cutting the ninety-ninth or ninety-eighth link also gets rid of the hundredth. Solve problems indirectly by using the following approaches:

- Solve Unsolvable Problem A in an unconventional way (untie the knot that can't be undone by cutting it open; when desiring to go from Europe to Asia when the easterly route is blocked, sail westward; when there is nowhere to store an unending flow of garbage, turn it into desirable building materials, fertilizer, and fuel).

- Solve Problem B making Unsolvable Problem A melt away or become insignificant (when we can't decide what color to dye our mustache, shaving it off removes the problem of choosing a dye color; when each month we have to decide between losing access to water or electricity due to a lack of money, taking a second job and increasing our income eliminates the unpleasant decision; if we must attend a meeting in a place where all air travel is suspended, turning our attention to alternatives like taking a train, driving, or sailing there, or attending the meeting via videoconference removes the need to solve the flight problem).

- Solve an indirectly related problem making several others disappear or become neutralized simultaneously (if we have ten money-related problems, becoming rich makes all ten fade away; if we have ten spouse-related problems, divorcing our spouse makes all ten trivial; if we have ten workplace-related problems, finding a new job or starting our own business makes all ten workplace problems dissipate).

- Make problems vanish into thin air by changing definitions and perceptions (if the traditional definition of a successful company is one which makes a profit each year and we're a company that loses lots of money, but our sales and market share are increasing each year, then changing the definition of a successful company to one which grows sales and market share magically makes us a successful company; turn a potentially dangerous loss into a win by convincing people it was really a "victory in disguise," if we convince the necessary people, then our loss truly does become a win; if Product X is considered by most people "low quality junk food," changing its definition to "health food" and its perception to "high quality," makes Product X "high quality health food" without making a single change to its ingredients).

SYSTEMATIZING

Just as organized is better than chaotic, practiced is better than unrehearsed, and planned is better than accidental, systematized is better than random. Systems are repeated tasks turned into well-organized routines. Systematized routines are more efficient than randomly executed tasks because they create mind and muscle memory and can be improved on through trial and error, resulting in better quality, increased quantity, and less resources spent; while randomly executed tasks result in random outcomes, sometimes good, sometimes not. Systematized routines are like rolling boulders downhill, while doing repeated tasks randomly is like rolling boulders uphill: which would you rather do? Define steps needed for completing our task, reduce them to only the most vital, then put them in their proper order; now, this is the only way we execute our task. Constantly attempt to improve our system (doing a little more, a little faster, a little better) by establishing a cycle of adjusting (only) one step at a time, evaluating the results after the change, then keeping the change or going back to the original way (before the change), depending on which is better. Systematize as many tasks as we can so effective efficiency becomes our habit.

RAISING AND RAZING HABITS

Building us up or tearing us down, habits are our best friends or worst enemies. Habits are reflexive routines occurring with little to no conscious effort; they're a loop of triggers, cravings, actions, and treats. Triggers stimulate our cravings for the treat and can be almost anything such as a certain time, place, person, emotion, or sensation. Cravings are subconscious pressures to possess the treat and these impulses push us to complete the action. Actions are the routines we must complete to receive our treat and are beneficial, neutral, or harmful. Treats are our reward for completing the action and can be anything that creates sensations of pleasure or satisfaction like good feelings after exercising, a sense of accomplishment after cleaning, enjoyable food and drink, money, or praise. Habits making us who we want to be and helping us achieve our goals are almost always deliberately designed, good habits rarely develop randomly. When we deliberately design productive and beneficial habits, we dramatically improve our chances of being who we want to be and achieving our goals; but when we don't deliberately design productive and beneficial habits, being who we want to be and achieving our goals is highly unlikely. Avoid developing unproductive and harmful habits because they can be ignored or replaced, but never fully erased. Consciously construct productive and beneficial (good) habits and deliberately avoid, ignore, or replace unproductive and harmful (bad) habits.

RAISING GOOD HABITS

Begin embedding our good habit by selecting the action we want to adopt, choose an action that helps make us who we want to be and moves us closer to achieving our goals. Now, convince ourselves the action is extremely advantageous and will benefit us greatly, this is the most important step in developing our new habit; if we believe the action is very valuable, we will adopt it; don't proceed until we want its benefits badly. Next, choose a simple and obvious trigger and create a connection between the trigger and the action; focus on the selected trigger, then immediately do the action (at exactly 7 a.m. we go to the gym; whenever we're at the beach, we go for a run on the sand; when our children return home from school, we immediately help them with their homework; when the fish tank begins to smell bad, we clean it; when we feel down, we visit our friends). Finally, give ourselves a (healthy) treat after completing the action (when we've completed our workout at the gym, we eat a delicious breakfast; after our run on the beach, we earn a runner's high; after helping our children with their homework, we feel like good parents; after cleaning the fish tank, we buy ourselves a new fish; after visiting our friends, our mood brightens). Make sure the treat is something we truly crave because our desire for the treat is our habit's fuel, the action won't become a habit without it. Consciously repeat this process until the trigger automatically creates a craving for the treat, and our craving for the treat immediately compels us to complete the action; when this happens, our habit is set.

RAZING BAD HABITS

Bad habits prevent us from being who we want to be and achieving our goals, they must be stopped. Stopping a bad habit requires commitment, perceived advantage, and willpower. Commitment is intending to follow through on our decision to stop our bad habit, perceived advantage is feeling stopping our bad habit is more beneficial than continuing it, and willpower is the ability to exercise discipline when craving our bad habit. Stop our bad habit today by making a firm commitment to stop it, convincing ourselves stopping is to our advantage, and using the following willpower aids to help stop it:

- Cut relations with anyone or anything triggering cravings for our bad habit. Sometimes this is realistic and doable, sometimes it's not.

- Contrast the small and short-lived satisfaction, thrill, and enjoyment derived from succumbing to our bad habit with the big disappointment, long-term discomfort, lost opportunities, and negative consequences suffered from succumbing to it. A few seconds, minutes, or hours of pleasure can't compare with days, months, or years of pain.

- Make each willpower moment a one-time event. Never think "I can't go the rest of my life without this!" Instead, think "I'm not going to do it this one time," we all have the willpower to not do something once, right? One "no" leads to many; and saying "no" once makes it easier to say "no" the next time.

- Keep score how long we've abstained from our bad habit and make it a prized possession. We hate losing valuable possessions, become attached to and proud of our bad habit-free number. Turn small daily wins into long-term success; the bigger the abstention number, the greater our attachment to it and the worse it feels losing it.

- Replace our bad habit with a good habit. When our cravings come, replace the bad action with a good action and then reward ourselves for doing the good action (we're craving alcohol or drugs, so we exercise or go fishing instead, then treat ourselves to a delicious meal; we want to chew on our fingers, but we chew gum instead and reward ourselves with a refreshing walk in the park; we desire chocolate cake for dessert, but eat fruit or drink juice, coffee, or tea instead, then praise ourselves "I did a great job, I'm very proud of myself").

Don't get discouraged if, most likely when, we succumb to cravings for our bad habit. Few things are harder than stopping a bad habit, but every bad habit can be stopped: don't give up. Willpower takes time to develop, but if we stay committed and remember the benefits, we will stop our bad habit.

BENEFICIAL LEARNING

The quality of our learning is far more important than the quantity, a little knowledge and know-how leading to productive action is far more valuable than lots of learning that gets us nowhere. Beneficial learning is learning knowledge (understood information) and know-how (mastered skills) leading to beneficial action. When we learn beneficial knowledge and know-how, we're prepared for beneficial action; but when we waste our time learning useless knowledge and know-how, we're not. Knowledge is power only when it leads to powerful action; when we can't do anything with it, knowledge is worthless. Identify what we need and want to do, then acquire the necessary knowledge and know-how to do it.

LEARNING KNOW-HOW

Modeling is learning skills and behaviors by copying those who have already mastered them. We learn best through imitation, and the most effective way to learn a skill or behavior is by imitating those doing it best. If we want to learn how to fish, we copy an expert fisherman; if we want to learn martial arts, we study with a master martial artist; and if we want good manners, we imitate those with the best manners. When we practice modeling, we learn skills and behaviors efficiently; and when we don't practice modeling, we may learn beneficial skills and behaviors, but we'll learn them inefficiently. If we're going to learn something, doesn't it make sense we learn it the best and easiest way? Identify our desired skill or behavior, then select the person we'll imitate. Next, isolate the actions making the person an expert and copy them. Never copy the entire person because we're all combinations of good and bad traits, imitate what makes us master our desired skill or behavior only and leave the rest.

Practicing is how skills are learned and mastered. The best practice is done with skilled instructors because we can use them as models; when we don't have access to trusted instructors, learn how to practice from videos and books. Remember, reading books isn't practicing; reading books teaches us how to practice, but isn't a replacement for it. Begin by selecting our desired skill, then commit to mastering it. Next, divide the skill into its core actions and fine details. Now, design our practice routines according to our skill level:

- Beginner's stage is where we become competent at the skill's core actions. Estimate how many hours of practice we'll need to become competent at the core actions (use 10-40 hours as a reference point), then divide the total hours into practice sessions of 20-90 minutes each. Finish the total hours as quickly as the skill (some skills can be practiced every day, some can't), our schedule (sometimes we have time to practice every day or twice a day, sometimes we don't), and our motivation (sometimes we're motivated to practice once or twice a day, sometimes we're not) allow. Beginner's stage is the most critical because frustration, due to a lack of progress, leads to lost confidence and enthusiasm causing many people to quit. To avoid this, get past beginner's stage, and into intermediate, as quickly as possible.

- Intermediate level is where we master the skill's core actions and become competent at its fine details. Estimate how many hours of practice we'll need to master the core actions and become competent at the fine details (use 10-60 hours as a reference point), then divide the total hours into practice sessions of 20-90 minutes each. Finish the total hours as quickly as the skill, our schedule, and our motivation allow. At intermediate level, consistency, sharpness, and precision are stressed over quickly getting to the advanced stage.

- Advanced stage is where we maintain mastery of the skill's core actions and master its fine details. Estimate how many hours of practice we'll need to maintain mastery of the core actions and to master the fine details (use 10-80 hours as a reference point), then divide the total hours into practice sessions of 20-90 minutes each. Finish the total hours as quickly as the skill, our schedule, and our motivation allow. Some skills take a long time to master, so determination and persistence are required to become experts.

- Experts maintain mastery of the skill's core actions and fine details while innovating new techniques. Estimate how many hours of practice we'll need each week or month to maintain mastery and innovate, then divide the total hours into practice sessions of 20-90 minutes each. If we don't keep practicing, our skills will erode; so, stay committed to consistent practice.

All practice sessions must be scheduled (set dates, starting and stopping times), hassle and friction-free (all mental and physical barriers to starting and completing practice session removed), and focused (once started, no interruptions or stopping until practice session is complete).

LEARNING KNOWLEDGE

Studying is how we learn recorded knowledge and begins by selecting quality source materials (what we'll listen to, watch, or read to learn our desired knowledge). Next, identify the important information from our source materials and concentrate our effort on learning it. Since images are easier to remember than sentences and paragraphs, turn our desired knowledge into mental pictures that cue our remembrance of it, then write notes that also help us remember it. Now, review our desired knowledge by memory. After reviewing it by memory, make it useful by contemplating its meaning, current applications, and potential uses. Finally, take a break from studying this subject and don't study it again until after we've rested (a full night's sleep or a short nap) to help our brain fully absorb it. Repeat this process until we've fully learned our desired knowledge. To ensure we learn it, make all study sessions scheduled, hassle and friction-free, and focused.

Experimenting is how we learn cause and effect relationships, leading to scientific discoveries and everyday knowledge of what happens when we do X and how to make Z happen. When experimenting, use the Scientific Method:

1. **Question** how or why something does or doesn't work, wonder what would happen if we did X or what makes Z happen, or doubt established cause and effect beliefs.

2. **Hypothesize**, or propose an answer to our question "We believe X causes Z." Hypotheses are based on previous observations, experiences, and data.

3. **Test** our hypothesis by running experiments. First, identify all variables involved with the occurrence of Z. Then, run a series of tests, removing/altering only one variable at a time, to see if Z still happens. When Z doesn't happen, then the missing/altered variable is its cause.

4. **Analyze**, or examine, the data (results of the test) to determine what they mean. Be objective because data can often be misread to mean anything we want.

5. **Conclude**, or decide, whether our original hypothesis is correct or incorrect (X causes Z or X does not cause Z).

USING KNOWLEDGE AND KNOW-HOW

Making is creating tangible and intangible objects for solving problems (wanting to cut meat and vegetables quicker, we make a knife; wanting to cross a river safer, we build a bridge; wanting to make a video game, we create a computer program). When making, use the Engineering Method:

1. **Explore** ideas for solving our problem.

2. **Design** a plan for solving our problem.

3. **Build** the solution to our problem.

4. **Test** what we've built to confirm it works properly.

5. **Improve** what we've built if it doesn't work properly.

Innovating is introducing completely new technologies (ways of doing things) or utilizing old technologies in completely new ways. Innovations come from exploring possibility's boundaries, examining applied solutions in unrelated industries, and exchanging ideas with industry enthusiasts. The easiest way to innovate is by (legally) using someone else's great idea and improving it, applying it to our industry, or just implementing it. Many great ideas are floating around unutilized because their originators don't know what to do with them or how to implement them. Both the people coming up with great ideas and the ones (legally) implementing them are innovators. When turning great ideas into reality, start by using the Engineering Method to build the most basic prototype possible, then improve it through iterations of one improvement at a time. An innovation nobody wants is worthless, so make people want our innovation by using persuasive influence (see Chapter 3).

Capitalizing on correctly perceived patterns and trends can change lives, create fortunes, and build dynasties. Patterns are rhythmically repeating actions or events (each day the Sun rises in the east and sets in the west, a new crescent moon can be seen every twenty-nine or thirty days, Boxer X always lowers his right hand before throwing his left) and trends are movements or shifts in a general direction (summers are getting hotter, the price of precious metals is falling, Population X is eating more beef and less rice). Seeing opportunities or dangers in patterns and trends before everyone else, then capitalizing on them, leads to hyper-advantage and windfall gains; but acting on incorrectly perceived, improperly understood patterns and trends exposes us to catastrophe. The problem with pursuing advantage in patterns and trends is there are so many ways and reasons our perceptions and understanding can be wrong, here are four:

1. **Perceived patterns may not really exist, and anticipated trends may never develop.** Sometimes, like a mirage, we see patterns that aren't really there; and sometimes what seems like a potentially huge wave ends up being a dud. If we're lucky, we catch our error before executing our capitalization plan; if not, we suffer the consequences.

2. **We attribute false causes to most outcomes.** Unless we can apply the Scientific Method, cause and effect is very difficult, if not impossible, to prove. We usually don't truly know why something happened like why Company X succeeded or failed, Candidate Z won or lost, or Idea Q was accepted or rejected. So, if we incorrectly believe Product X is successful because it has Z, then based on our incorrect understanding we invest heavily in a new product featuring Z, we suffer a devastating loss when it fails.

3. **Almost all historical events are inaccurately recorded.** Extracting useful patterns and trends from them is tricky for the following reasons:

    - History is written, and rewritten, by the victors glorifying and legitimizing their group and their group's heroes and villainizing and delegitimizing their enemy's group and heroes; historical accuracy is not their goal.

    - Human memory is extremely fallible, many reports of events given by honest people were unintentionally false.

    - Most interpretations of historical events (their causes, consequences, and significance) are probably wrong because we generally can't test historical events with the Scientific Method.

4. **Well-established patterns and trends are not guaranteed to continue.** Just because something has happened ninety-nine times doesn't guarantee it will happen the hundredth, and just because something has continued happening for a thousand years doesn't mean it will continue happening from this point forward. By the time we begin executing our capitalization plan, the pattern or trend could have already ended.

Constantly watch for undiscovered patterns and emerging trends. When perceived, confirm they're genuine and properly understood. After confirmation, immediately plan beneficial actions, then swiftly act.

5
HEALTHY RELATIONSHIPS

And your Lord has decreed you worship none but Him and you be kind to your parents; if one or both of them attain old age, don't speak to them disrespectfully and don't chide or repulse them, but speak to them honorably. Lower to them, out of compassion, the wing of submission and humility and say, "My Lord, have mercy on them as they took care of me when I was young."

—The Qur'an 17:23-24 (translation)

HEALTHY LIVING

Some illnesses are beyond our control, but many—like depression, obesity, and pollution-related illnesses—are preventable or curable with healthy living. Healthy living is taking responsibility for our mental, physical, and environmental health; we can't wish our way to being healthy; there are no magic pills or potions granting good health; and our parents, teachers, and doctors can teach us how to live healthy, but no one can do it for us. When we take responsibility for our health, we're guaranteed the best health destiny permits; but when we don't, we'll probably end up with health problems we could've avoided. Our health is too valuable to neglect or leave to chance; for ourselves, our loved ones, and our dependents, choose healthy living today. Healthy living requires a healthy mind, body, healing, and Earth.

HEALTHY MIND

Develop and maintain a healthy mind by cultivating consistency, self-worth, mental toughness, proper expectations, effort, belief in destiny, self-forgiveness, and hope (see Chapter 1). Living consistently with our principles establishes and confirms our identity, purpose, and meaning; self-worth gives us the self-love and self-respect we so desperately need; mental toughness provides us the mental strength to cope with all difficulties; proper expectations allow us to be satisfied with natural and realistic conditions and situations; giving our sincerely best effort assures us the best destiny possible; belief in destiny allows us to accept and deal with non-optimal outcomes; self-forgiveness helps us overcome our mistakes, failures, and unfulfilled aspirations; and hope in a better and brighter future fuels our perseverant "never give up" spirit. Together, they create internal peace, harmony, and well-being, the benefits of a healthy mind. Also, never allow fearful, disturbing, or disgusting thoughts, feelings, or desires to negatively affect our mental health. Involuntary thoughts, feelings, and desires are very common; neither feel scared nor guilty because of them. Prevent or cure fear, guilt, and distress caused by involuntary thoughts, feelings, and desires with the following mental health fixes:

- **Believe only actions can be bad.** If we involuntarily think about, crave, or desire something bad, but don't act on these impulses, nothing bad has happened.

- **Believe we have total control over our actions.** If we involuntarily think about, crave, or desire something bad, we have the power not to do it.

- **Believe irrational thoughts can't happen.** If it can't happen, then don't worry about it.

- **Be brave.** Fearful thoughts go away when we conquer our fears.

HEALTHY BODY

A healthy body begins with a nutritious diet. A nutritious diet gives our body the energy it needs for optimal performance and maintains our prime body weight. There's no single type of nutritious diet, a nutritious diet could include no meat or almost all meat. What all nutritious diets have in common is they provide our necessary vitamins and minerals, make us feel strong and energetic, and equalize our calorie intake and calories burned. The following tips help us eat a nutritious diet:

- **Neither stuff nor starve ourselves.** Eating past the point of satisfaction packs on the pounds, and extreme dieting leaves us feeling weak, food-crazy, and vulnerable to losing control.

- **Avoid empty calories.** Empty calories are foods high in calories but low in nutritional value like cookies, cakes, candies, ice cream, potato chips, and sodas.

- **Learn to like most vegetables.** Getting all our vitamins and minerals is much easier when we like vegetables.

- **Choose the healthier dessert option.** When craving sweets, eat fruits (fresh, canned, dried) or drink fruit juice, coffee, or tea. Coffee or tea sweetened with honey or sugar does far less damage than cookies, cakes, and candies.

- **Go to sleep on an (almost) empty stomach.** Eating dinner at least three hours before sleep gives our body time to digest our food.

- **Never eat as a cure for sadness or depression.** Fix sadness and depression with a healthy mind (see earlier section).

A healthy body also requires lots of exercise. Exercise is physical activity which stimulates our cardiovascular system, develops muscle strength and flexibility, and improves posture and balance. The four main exercise categories are cardiovascular, resistance, stretching, and balance. Cardiovascular exercises (running, swimming, biking) strengthen our heart and lungs, build endurance, and burn tons of calories; resistance exercises (push-ups, sit-ups, weightlifting) strengthen muscles; stretching exercises (trunk twists, shoulder rolls, toe touches) make muscles flexible; and balance exercises (standing on one foot, rail walking, martial arts training) develop posture, stability, and coordination. Blend these four exercise categories into effective exercise routines by following these tips:

- **Make exercising our habit.** Exercise makes us feel good and look great, learn to desire and crave these benefits.

- **Make exercising our hobby, not a chore**. There are an endless number of exercises to choose from, blend together the ones we enjoy most.

- **Make exercise routines consistent and varied**. For instance, exercise every day; every other day; or two days exercise, one day off; and one exercise session run, the next session lift weights, and the following session practice martial arts.

- **Embrace intensity while avoiding injuries**. Push ourselves (almost) to the limit, and if we habitually become injured, change how we do the exercise, lower the intensity, or switch to a different exercise.

- **Do a complete body stretch every day**. Stretching makes muscles flexible and prevents injuries; always stretch before exercising and also on our rest days.

- **Walk as fast, far, and often as we can**. Don't allow sexier exercises like running, weightlifting, and martial arts training to make us underestimate walking's benefits; walking is the highest value, lowest cost (in terms of injuries) exercise there is, take advantage of it.

A healthy body consistently rests sufficiently. Resting isn't a waste of time, but essential like eating, drinking, and breathing; while resting, our body heals, refreshes, and recharges. Tasks, projects, and goals can't be completed efficiently without enough rest—and though we may get by with little to no rest for a while—we'll suffer without it long-term. Rest sufficiently by observing the following rest routines:

- **Sleep no less than five, and no more than eight, hours daily**. Everyone's body is different, but less than five hours sleep is definitely not enough, and unless sick or injured, more than eight hours sleep is probably too much.

- **Nap for a half hour every afternoon**. Set a timer for thirty minutes, then unplug and disconnect; don't answer phone calls, check messages, or answer the door. Lay down, close our eyes, and relax; even if we don't fall asleep, our body and mind will be refreshed.

- **Take breaks, while working and from working**. While working, take a 10 to 20-minute break every 50-90 minutes that's disconnected from work; preferably, with other people and surrounded by nature. When not working, completely disconnect from work, relax, and unwind with family, friends, and enjoyable hobbies.

Finally, a healthy body observes good hygiene. Observing good hygiene is our best defense against pathogens, harmful microorganisms that make us sick. We can prevent most sicknesses caused by pathogens by keeping our body, clothes, working and living areas clean and neat. Beware, being clean is good, but being a germaphobe is bad: don't go overboard. Observe good hygiene with the following good hygiene habits:

- Touch our mouth, eyes, ears, nose, and open wounds with extremely clean hands only.

- Keep our body and clothes urine, feces, blood, mucous, and saliva free (human and animal).

- Keep our working and living areas urine, feces, blood, mucous, saliva, dust, and clutter free.

- Abstain from eating unwashed fruits and vegetables, raw meat and seafood, and drinking unpurified water.

- Brush and floss our teeth at least once a day, but preferably after every meal; if brushing and flossing after every meal isn't practical, then rinse our mouth thoroughly after each food and drink contact.

HEALTHY HEALING

Even with an extremely nutritious diet, rigorous exercise, sufficient sleep, and good hygiene, we'll still need healing; when we do, turn to home remedies first (bed rest, honey, lemon tea, massage) and doctors and prescribed medicines second. Doctors and prescribed medicines are vital for living healthy, but an overreliance on them is dangerous. Doctors can give misdiagnoses with harmful consequences; medicines, including herbal medicines, can have damaging side-effects; and since most illnesses require bed rest only, visiting doctors and taking prescription medication should be our second option, not our first. Be careful, home remedies won't cure cataracts, rabies, or a burst appendix; when doctors and prescribed medicines are required, seek treatment immediately. Also, home remedies are not a substitute for vaccines. Vaccines dramatically reduce our risk of becoming permanently disabled or dying from infectious diseases. Vaccinated societies trade thousands upon thousands of people becoming sick or dying from preventable infectious diseases for dozens of people becoming sick or dying from allergic reactions to vaccines: only a fool wouldn't take that deal. Get all vital vaccines (like Polio) as prescribed, and the optional vaccines (like the Flu) are exactly that, optional.

HEALTHY EARTH

A clean home, free of toxins, is necessary for healthy living. The Earth is our home, and our health depends on its fresh air, pure water, and fertile soil. Without them, we can't be healthy, so preserving them for ourselves and our descendants is a must. Zero waste living—the elimination of trash by composting, reusing, and recycling everything—preserves our fresh air, pure water, and fertile soil while allowing us to enjoy all the comforts of modernity. Initially, zero waste living may seem impossible, but it's very doable; for the average person, it requires only a few new habits. If we commit, individually and collectively, to zero waste living, we'll preserve our fresh air, pure water, and fertile soil; but if we don't, we'll make our air smoggy, water poisonous, and soil toxic. Our current lifestyle is unsustainable; if we keep producing garbage at our current rate, we'll make the whole Earth one huge trash dump very soon. Start protecting our planet's resources today with the following zero waste living fixes:

- Individually and collectively, commit to composting, reusing, and recycling everything.

- Mandate all pollution be cleaned up completely by the polluter. If fifty billion dollars of pollution is created, then the polluter must spend fifty billion dollars cleaning it up, not one penny less.

- Include recycling costs at the point of sale, so when it's time to recycle it'll feel "free."

- Close all trash dumps, clean them up, and put them to productive uses.

FULFILLING RELATIONSHIPS

During our lifetime, we fulfill multiple relationship roles: son or daughter, brother or sister, husband or wife, father or mother, friend, neighbor, classmate, co-worker, and citizen. Each relationship role carries its own unique rights and responsibilities whose fulfilment is required for social harmony. Being rude to our parents, cutting relations with siblings, abusing spouses, abandoning children, betraying friends, fighting with neighbors, slandering classmates, backstabbing co-workers, and terrorizing fellow citizens destroys social harmony and results in a society of broken relationships. So, whether we want to or not, we must fulfill our relationship roles. When we fulfill our relationship roles, we create a harmonious society, but when we don't, we create a broken society. Being free and living as we wish is great, but when it destroys our society, it's sinful. Begin by setting a goal of being the best child, sibling, spouse, parent, friend, neighbor, classmate, co-worker, and citizen ever. Even "when" we don't achieve this goal, our relationships will be as good as they can be. Then, be respectful with everyone by not hurting their feelings or making them feel uncomfortable. Putting down others doesn't increase our status and joking or teasing that hurts people's feelings or makes them uncomfortable isn't funny, it's cruel. Next, give everyone the attention they need. Never leave anyone starving for praise, appreciation, sympathy, or encouragement. Tell those we love "I love you," those we care about "I care about you," those we appreciate "I appreciate all you do for me," those who need encouragement "I believe in you," those who deserve congratulations "You did a great job, I'm very proud of you," and return every kindness, small or great, with a smile and "thank you." Help solve their problems, if we can, and console them when they're down. Also, be trustworthy by keeping everyone's secrets secret. The closer our relationship, the more we know each other's "dirty laundry." It's our responsibility to keep these things hidden. Using other's secrets as weapons against them or gossip is dishonorable, don't do it. Of course, active crimes like spousal abuse, serial killing, and child molestation can never be covered up; instead, they must be stopped immediately, and secrets that harm others (such as the fiancé of Woman A claims to be faithful but is truly a serial fornicator, Man A is lying about his upstanding character when vying for a leadership position, or we're certain our neighbor's child is using drugs) must be exposed. Plus, make forgiveness our default setting. We all do and say offensive things (both unintentionally and on purpose), if we're unwilling to forgive, then we'll never have a long-term relationship with anyone. Forgiving others is usually to our advantage, so when the offense isn't too great, and the person is genuinely sorry, and we're fairly certain it won't happen again, then forgive. Never forgive offenses that cross red lines, aren't genuinely regretted, or leave us exposed to further harm. With these general relationship rules in mind, fulfill the following relationship roles:

CHILD

Children must always respect their parents. As young children, we respect our parents by obeying them and never being rude to them. Obeying our parents means doing what they tell us to do and not doing what they tell us not to do; never being rude to them means not talking back, rolling our eyes, raising our voices in anger, or ignoring them. As adults, we're not obligated to obey our parents, but we're still obligated to never be rude to them; plus, we're obligated to be kind to them and to take care of them as they were kind and took care of us. Copy all the good things they do, forgive them of any bad things they do, and learn lessons from their bad actions by doing the opposite. Treat our grandparents, aunts, and uncles similar to how we treat our parents.

SIBLING

After our parents, make our most trusted allies our siblings. Do everything we reasonably can to help them; and when we need advice, encouragement, or help, (after our parents) turn to them first. Keep our relationships with our siblings strong by avoiding rivalry, jealousy, and grudges. Make our bonds with our cousins similar to our bonds with our siblings.

SPOUSE

Being the best spouse ever begins with selecting an appropriate mate. Define our desired lifestyle, then marry someone who helps us live it or at least won't prevent us from living it. Never marry someone who'll split us from our family or principles; and never, never, never, pursue or accept someone solely because we're attracted to them. Attraction and desire don't make happy, productive marriages—love does—and attraction and desire aren't the same as love. We may not have control over who we're attracted to and desire, but we do have total control over who we pursue and accept in marriage; only pursue and accept appropriate mates. The best spousal relationships are mutually beneficial, "I do for you, you do for me" relationships where both spouses do their best to make each other happy and satisfied: this is love. Decisions are made together with the best interests of the family taking precedence over personal wants; responsibilities (who supplies the money, shops for groceries, does the laundry) are clearly and specifically defined and agreed upon; and emotional support filled with tenderness, compassion, and encouragement is enthusiastically supplied. When making love, hot, passionate sex—which fulfills the physical and emotional needs of both spouses and leaves both feeling loved, appreciated, and satisfied—is the goal. Our brain is our most important sexual organ; it's where hot, passionate sex begins and ends, so aim to please it. Approach our spouse with natural and realistic expectations; be content with our spouse and focus on what we like about them; remember, we make love to real and complete human beings, not fantasies and not legs, breasts, butts, or penises. Make our spouse feel accepted, comfortable, and desired. Find out what they like and do it; kiss them where they want to be kissed, touch them where they want to be touched, and most importantly, tell them what they want to hear. High energy and enthusiasm are a must. Consume all their sexual desire, every last drop, then reassure them with praise, compliments, and appreciation ("That was the best sex ever, thank you," "I love you more than any man has ever loved a woman before," "If I could pick any woman in the world, I'd pick you"). Avoid being cold and aloof, insulting when angry, and holding on to resentments and grudges. Also, never accept exploitation, abuse, or neglect; either the exploitation, abuse, and neglect end or the marriage does.

PARENT

As parents, raise our children with equal parts discipline and affection. Discipline is establishing and enforcing rules and boundaries; affection is making our children feel loved, wanted, and cared for. Raising our children with equal parts discipline and affection gives them their best chance of becoming responsible, self-assured, successful adults because raising them with mostly discipline usually leads to them feeling unloved, unwanted, and uncared for; and raising them with all affection usually results in them becoming spoiled, selfish, and ungrateful. No matter how badly we want our children to be successful, too much discipline isn't the solution; and no matter how much we want them to love us, too much affection isn't the solution; equal parts discipline and affection is the proper course. When our children are adults, advise, but never try controlling them; adults must be allowed to be adults. Make our relationships with our grandchildren, nieces, and nephews like our relationships with our children. Also, make women the primary caretakers of children. The uncomfortable truth is most physical, and almost all sexual abuse of children is carried out by men; therefore, the natural solution is for men not to be left alone with them. Despite many women being disrespected and made to feel ashamed because their primary job is childcare, childcare is the most honorable and important job a woman can do. Just as a surgeon could be a great carpenter but shouldn't because he's more needed by his community as a surgeon, a woman qualified for a thousand other jobs is needed most as a caretaker of children. When women are the primary caretakers of children, children's safety is maximized; while leaving young children unsupervised with men is like leaving lambs alone with wolves. Of course, most men are good and would never dream of harming children; but since we don't know which men are monsters until it's too late, only women are qualified to supervise our children. Put women in charge of young children 24/7; make them their babysitters, teachers, and doctors; ensure every man interacting with young children has a woman's eye on him at all times; and give women the respect and compensation due for fulfilling such a critical role.

FRIEND

Great friendships are based on shared interests and goals. A good friend is trustworthy, helpful, and respectful; a bad friend is the opposite. Choose friends wisely because bad friends probably will make us bad. Define our desired lifestyle, then select friends that help us live this lifestyle. Also, avoid being desperate for friendship; desperation is unattractive and usually repels potential good friends while attracting con artists and exploiters. Be a good friend, choose only good friends, cut relations with bad friends, and never forget family relationships take precedence over friendships.

HEALTHY RELATIONSHIPS

NEIGHBOR, CLASSMATE, CO-WORKER, AND CITIZEN

Goodwill, courtesy, and cooperation are needed for harmonious relationships with our neighbors, classmates, co-workers, and fellow citizens. "Do no harm" is our binding agreement with them; plus, we band together to protect each other from those viewing us as prey. Small groups of family, friends, neighbors, classmates, co-workers, and fellow citizens stop individual bullies and criminals; while large groups stop gangs of them; the good guys must be braver and more violent than the bad guys. When able, help our needy neighbors, classmates, co-workers, and fellow citizens; don't leave them hungry, cold, wet, and homeless while we're full, warm, dry, and comfortable; if we can help them but don't, then who will? Be aware that male and female neighbors, classmates, co-workers, and fellow citizens (non-relatives) can't be "just friends." It's natural to view each other, consciously or subconsciously, as potential mates; so, when men and women spend time together it usually results in at least one desiring the other. History proves this; therefore, all our interactions with the opposite sex must have this in mind. Also, men must embrace their role as supporters and protectors of women and reject the dishonorable and shameful practice of using and abusing women. A man's prestige doesn't come from how many women he penetrates or how much he takes from them; rather, it comes from how many women he supports and protects. No man wants his mother, sister, daughter, or wife to be sexually harassed and exploited, used financially, or mentally and physically abused; so, how can we do this to our friend's, neighbor's, classmate's, co-worker's, or fellow citizen's mother, sister, daughter, or wife? Let's be "real men" and support and protect all women.

MAN/WOMAN

Finally, for a harmonious society, men must be men and women must be women. Men are masculine, acting and dressing like men; women are feminine, acting and dressing like women. Men are sensitive, caring, and compassionate, but in a masculine way; women are strong, tough, and fearless, but in a feminine way. Men marry women and women marry men; this isn't hate, it's how the world must work. No one can deny some men are attracted to and desire other men and some women are attracted to and desire other women, and no one can deny some men desperately want to be women and some women desperately want to be men, but feelings and desires never justify inappropriate behavior. Rapists, child molesters, and serial killers have undeniable feelings and desires; but we all agree their feelings and desires can never be acted upon. No matter what our feelings and desires may be, men must be men, women must be women, men must marry only women, and women must marry only men. This is how the world must work.

6
WARFARE LEADERSHIP

Let those fight in the cause of Allah who sell the life of this world for the hereafter, and whoever fights in the cause of Allah, slain or victorious, We will give them a great reward. What's wrong with you that you don't fight in the cause of Allah and for the weak, ill-treated, and oppressed men, women, and children who cry, "Our Lord, rescue us from this town whose people are oppressors, and raise for us, from Yourself, a protector and helper."

—The Qur'an 4:74-75 (translation)

INSPIRING LEADERSHIP

Every purpose-based group (family, business, religion) needs an inspiring leader. Inspiring leaders arouse belief in their vision of success, unify supporters' loyalty to this vision, and direct supporters' resources towards achieving this vision. Groups with inspiring leaders can achieve their goals, groups without inspiring leaders can't. Be aware of the difference between inspiring leaders and con artists: inspiring leaders call towards a better and brighter future for their supporters—be an inspiring leader or support inspiring leaders, while con artists abuse their leadership positions for self-enrichment—never be or support a con artist. Arouse belief with an attractive, simple, and doable vision that promises a better and brighter future, is summed up in one or two phrases, and is generally accepted as achievable. Generate interest and enthusiasm by touching hearts with messages of 80% emotion and 20% logic. Blend the past, present, and future into one glorious outcome; explain who we are, where we come from, how we got here, where we need to go, and that our vision is the only way we'll get there. When we arouse belief, our supporters will move mountains to make our vision reality. After belief is aroused, unify our supporters' loyalty to our group by rallying them around our vision's achievement. Make our supporters feel our group is their family, a rightly guided community shaping the world as it should be. Bind their identity, purpose, and meaning with our group's principles, and make them view their success and our group's success as one. Our supporters must love our group, feel they need it, and fear losing their connection to it. Establish symbols (actions, words, dress) that foster and reinforce feelings of community, belonging, and commitment. When loyalty is unified, thousands, millions, or even billions of people can act as one. Once we have a unified, loyal group of supporters, maximize our potential by directing our group's resources wisely. Persuade our supporters to willingly donate their resources (time, energy, money) for the good of the group, then concentrate these resources towards what most efficiently makes our vision reality. Delegate responsibilities based on merit, don't push our supporters past their capacities, and never ask them to do what we wouldn't. Share in their hardships; be the first to sacrifice, the first to "feel the pain." After our supporters believe, view themselves and our group as one, and sacrifice their resources for the good of our group, we persist and persevere until our vision becomes reality.

WINNING WARFARE

War is collective violence, or the threat of it, for seizing and protecting advantage. War is not separate from politics; rather, it's one option in our political toolbox. Being skilled and dedicated to winning warfare enables us to protect our citizens, preserve our culture, and project our principles; while not being committed to winning warfare exposes our citizens and culture to conquest, exploitation, and annihilation. In both blood and treasure, waging war is very expensive; our best and brightest are killed, our women violated, and our assets exhausted, all with no guarantee of victory; make war the last option for getting what we want, not the first.

WIN THE WAR AND THE PEACE

Before the war begins, clearly and specifically define what we want and make these the terms we force our enemy to accept, this alone is true victory. Also, never give up our advantage by allowing our enemy to stall for time with promises of a peace treaty; don't stop fighting until a peace treaty is signed. Finally, no one honors a peace treaty we can't enforce; if we're left wishing and hoping it's honored, then don't accept it.

TARGET DECISION MAKERS

Winning warfare is not defeating armies (avoid armies unless engagement is advantageous or necessary); instead, win wars by making our enemy's decision makers lose their will to resist. Take away their access to food, clothing, shelter, water, power, transportation, commerce, and entertainment; consume and destroy their wealth; eliminate their feelings of safety and security; separate them from their homes, families, and friends; and kill them and their supporters. Make our enemy's decision makers feel peace with us, on our terms, is preferable to continued conflict. Utilize only strategy and tactics consistent with our society's principles; never torture or rape anyone and don't intentionally kill civilians.

WAR IS DECEPTION

Confuse, mislead, and surprise our enemy in all aspects of war through misinformation, trickery, and unpredictability. When few, seem many; when near, seem far; when strong, seem weak. Through propaganda, win hearts and minds, spread fear and confusion, and ruin our enemy's plans. Split our enemy from his allies, his soldiers from their commanders, and his citizens from their leaders. Have our agents sabotage his economy, plant false stories, and stir up internal opposition. Use peace talks as a delay tactic, but once a peace treaty is made, never break it.

KNOWLEDGE IS POWER

Know seasons, weather, climate, terrain, time, and distance. To discover our enemy's weaknesses, know his culture—history, language, religion, and customs—along with his capabilities, movements, and plans. Also, use this knowledge for turning his strengths into weaknesses, neutralizing them, or avoiding them. Almost all knowledge of our enemy comes from spies, so invest significant resources into building and maintaining spy networks composed of our enemy's government and military officials, their staff and attendants, common citizens, and double agents; jealously guard our spies' identities. Leave our enemy unprepared by keeping our capabilities, movements, and plans concealed through secrecy, misinformation, and stealth.

A HUMAN'S GUIDE FOR EVERYDAY LIFE

MAKE THE RIGHT MOVE AT THE RIGHT TIME

Be first; first to move, arrive, and strike. Be unexpected; take unorthodox paths, arrive and hit when and where we're unanticipated. Attack weakness (unprepared, divided, poorly defended) and avoid strength (prepared, concentrated, well-defended). Distract then surprise; never directly attack a prepared enemy, attack in unpredictable waves of distraction assaults which set up decisive surprise strikes. Offer baits to entice; fake terror, disorder, and flight, lure our enemy where we want him and strike. Make him believe we're going to attack Point A, making him defend it, then attack a weakly guarded Point B. Threaten several points simultaneously forcing our enemy to decide which to defend and how to defend them, then attack weakness. Move our enemy from a point of strength by threatening or attacking what he must defend. Target flanks and rear; target enemy's sides (flanks) and back (rear) to create apprehension, confusion, and terror; especially target his rear to cut lines of supplies, communications, reinforcements, and retreat. Harass and demoralize; hit with quick rear and flank ambushes or night raids, then swiftly disappear; give our enemy no rest, recovery, or peace of mind. Divide and conquer; split enemy, then defeat one party before the other can assist; defeat a larger group by attacking their divided forces with our concentrated forces.

SUPERIOR TECHNOLOGY CREATES ADVANTAGE

Master S.T.E.M. (science, technology, engineering, and mathematics) for innovating or adopting new tools, equipment, and weapons. Cutting-edge technology can change outcomes; at the least, our technology must be comparable to our enemy's because sticks and stones can't beat jets and missiles. Detest and shun sloppy and lazy lifestyles that avoid the dirty hands, strained brains, and precision necessary for designing, constructing, and using cutting-edge technology. Also, never be complacent with our current technology because what was effective yesterday isn't guaranteed to be effective today.

MANAGE SOLDIERS WISELY

Make our citizens want to be soldiers by honoring military service and ensuring it leads to better job and marital opportunities. Plus, make martyrdom our society's highest honor so every citizen desires to be a martyr or be related to a martyr. Have recruits sign a service agreement with all rights and responsibilities clearly and specifically defined, then have them take a pledge of allegiance. Train them to willingly embrace fatigue, hardship, and danger; pursue only three options when fighting: victory, strategic retreat, or martyrdom; and view surrender, with its accompanying indignities and tortures, as taboo. Feed, clothe, and equip soldiers to the best of our ability; treat them with equal parts discipline and affection; and don't ask them to kill themselves intentionally as weapons of war; never waste our soldiers' lives unnecessarily.

7
GOVERNING JUSTLY

And We ordained for them therein a life for a life, an eye for an eye, a nose for a nose, an ear for an ear, a tooth for a tooth, and wounds equal for equal, but if anyone charitably remits the retaliation it's for them atonement: whoever does not judge by what Allah has revealed, they are unjust.

—The Qur'an 5:45 (translation)

We all want to be governed justly, but we're not, and our efforts to be governed justly are in vain. We're stuck in a vicious cycle of replacing bad leaders and governments with worse; we're frustrated, furious, and fed up; we want to end unjust governance now. The first step to ending unjust governance is defining just governance. The just government exists solely for its citizens' benefit. Its leaders are elected by its citizens for short terms, governs by the majority-group's principles, and its citizens achieve based on merit. It values personal freedom, personal responsibility, and hands up are provided, but no handouts. Local governance, community policing, equal and swift justice, and zero jailing are preferred. When governed justly, societies develop, improve, and grow; but when not governed justly, they stagnate, deteriorate, and decline. Governance has been done incorrectly for almost all of human history, used by a few ruling elites for extracting society's wealth; lets fix this now with just governance. Just governments regulate society by the following principles:

GOVERNMENT EXISTS SOLELY FOR CITIZENS' BENEFIT

Government's role is implementing its citizens' will, "citizens' will" meaning the majority-group's principles, needs, and aspirations; all government laws and endeavors must have this as the end-goal. Government's role is not taking its citizens' wealth, creating cushy jobs for the ruling class, or making laws and pursuing endeavors beneficial only for those governing.

CITIZENS ELECT THEIR LEADERS

Citizens electing their leaders, for short terms, is the only way to guarantee leaders represent their citizens' principles, needs, and aspirations, because leaders who don't are replaced. Monarchs and dictators aren't elected and have no term limits, so they govern for their own self-enrichment; while elected leaders governing too long turn into dictators and monarchs because the longer power is held, the harder it is to give up.

GOVERNMENT BASED ON MAJORITY-GROUP'S PRINCIPLES

Harmony demands all laws and endeavors reflect the majority-group's beliefs, values, and goals. When the majority-group is governed by minority-group principles or their principles are sacrificed to make minorities feel comfortable, they naturally feel angry and resentful; this endangers minority-group prospects for long-term safety, stability, and prosperity. When minority-group customs don't violate the majority-group's principles, they're free to live as they wish; but when principles and customs conflict, minorities must adjust.

MERIT-BASED ACHIEVEMENT

Just governments respect positions earned by talent, courage, and determination, and despise positions achieved through cheating, bribery, and inheritance. Positions go to the most qualified because this allows society to flourish and thrive; positions are never given based on lineage or class because this results in less capable people dragging society down. Provide all citizens lifelong access to a first-class education, training, and retraining, then let the cream rise to the top.

PERSONAL FREEDOM

Freedom is required for development, improvement, and growth, so it's the just government's default setting. Everything is presumed permissible unless proven otherwise, meaning no one can be stopped from doing anything unless it clearly violates society's principles or another citizen's rights; actions lying in grey areas can't be prohibited and are left to personal choice and conscience. Also, freedom is never sold for promises of safety because freedom is superior to safety, safety can't be guaranteed, and giving up some freedom is the first step to losing it all.

PERSONAL RESPONSIBILITY

Just governments strive to implement their citizens' will, but never parent them. Each individual citizen is responsible for his own finances, health, safety, and family because freedom and a "nanny state" aren't compatible. Responsible financial, health, safety, and parenting practices can be recommended by government, but never mandated.

HANDS UP, NOT HANDOUTS

Citizens are society's most valuable assets; skilled and capable individuals make society stable, dynamic, and rich. Just governments invest in their growth by providing lifelong opportunities for a first-class education, training, and retraining. Plus, everyone willing to work, or incapable of working, is guaranteed basic food, clothing, and shelter; allowing our fellow citizens to be homeless, cold, and hungry is shameful; and never forget, we're all just one bad event away from being homeless, cold, and hungry. Those not desiring further training and those able but unwilling to work are given nothing.

LOCAL GOVERNANCE

The same solution doesn't work everywhere; local governments know best their problems and what solutions will work in their localities, that's why just governments rely on local governments for satisfying citizens' needs. Local governments inform central governments of citizens' needs, central governments set big-picture objectives, and local governments make them happen as appropriate to local conditions and capabilities.

COMMUNITY POLICING

A police department's job is protecting and serving its community, this is done best by local community members. Local community members are more likely to care deeply about the community's safety; view its citizens in a positive light; and treat them with compassion, dignity, and respect. Outsiders policing a community often view that community, especially if it's poor or minority, as a dangerous threat needing to be contained, controlled, and subdued; act like the community's jailors; and harass, abuse, and exploit them. Police must prefer death to harming an innocent citizen; in return, citizens must respect and honor police, with harassing, threatening, or harming them taboo.

EQUAL AND SWIFT JUSTICE

In societies governed justly, laws apply to everyone equally regardless of financial status, class, and connections. The rich and powerful aren't allowed to break laws with impunity and the law isn't used as a weapon for bullying minorities or stealing rich citizens' property. Also, court cases don't last more than a few months—including the initial charge, trial, and appeal—because citizens can't afford the time, worry, and money years-long court cases consume. A high bar for conviction (several witnesses and pieces of evidence) prevents wrongful convictions, punishments are implemented immediately after final appeal, and compensation is paid to anyone later proven innocent.

ZERO JAILING

Finally, just governments don't imprison their citizens because jails are expensive and difficult to operate; it leads to mistreatment, abuse, and exploitation of prisoners; and results in ex-prisoners more inclined to future crimes, not less. Punishments—fines, community service, whippings, amputations, and executions—are easier, cheaper, and at the least, as effective as jailing. Some believe punishments are cruel and inhumane, but we believe jailing people for years and decades is far crueler and inhumane: humans don't belong in cages. All societies need deterrents, but we believe jailing is not the deterrent used by a just government.

8
INVITING HUMANITY TO SUCCESS

Those who believed in Our signs and were Muslims, enter Paradise, you and your spouses: you will be made happy. Passed round to them are golden plates and cups, and there is all that souls desire and eyes delight in, and you will live there forever.

—The Qur'an 43:69-71 (translation)

Do you want to be content? Do you want to know the meaning of life? Do you want to be eternally successful? Follow me and, God willing, I'll guide you to all this. Contentment, knowledge of the meaning of life, and eternal success come from one source only: Islam. Islam's principles provide our identity, purpose, and meaning; Islam teaches who we are, where we come from, how we got here, and where we need to go; and Islam prepares us for the eternal success of Paradise. We all come from Allah, He is the creator and sustainer of all existence; destiny and power lie in His hands alone; He gives life and causes death; allows or prevents happiness, sadness, success, and failure; He has no parents, children, spouses, partners, competitors, or rivals; Allah is the only true god. He commands us to worship Him alone, as Muslims, and to make Islam our society's way of life. In the beginning, Allah made humans Earth's leaders, ordained Islam as our religion and way of life, and gave us free will to accept or reject it. He tests us with happiness and sadness, wealth and poverty, good health and bad, to discover if we're grateful and faithful. Allah sent prophets to deliver His message of Islam; Adam, Noah, Abraham, Moses, and Jesus (may peace and blessings be upon them) were all prophets of Allah who practiced and preached the same religion: Islam. Allah's final prophet of Islam, the prophet we must follow today, is the prophet Muhammad (may peace and blessings be upon him). We follow the book Allah gave him (the Qur'an), obey his teachings, and use him as our role model. At a time and date known by Allah alone, this world will end, the dead will be raised, and Allah will gather all humanity—the first to the last—for the Day of Judgement; on that day, all our beliefs and actions will be presented to us in a book and our good deeds will be weighed against our bad. If we make Islam our religion and way of life, then Allah rewards us with eternal bliss in Paradise, where every craving and desire is fulfilled forever; but for those who reject Islam as their religion and way of life, Allah punishes them with Hell, a place of never-ending and unbearable torture. I can't prove this empirically; I can't show you Allah, His angels, His prophets, Paradise, or Hell, but I can guide you to the Qur'an. If you approach it with a pure heart, I believe you will feel its truth and embrace Islam. It's true other belief systems can provide contentment in this world and (false) knowledge of the meaning of life; but only Islam gives us contentment in this world, knowledge of the true meaning of life, and eternal success: the inexhaustible pleasures of Paradise and safety from the unbearable tortures of Hell. Please, make Islam your religion and way of life today. Making Islam our religion and way of life is a three-step process of accepting, learning, and living Islam.

ACCEPTING ISLAM

1. Accept the declaration of faith "I bear witness there is no god but Allah, and I bear witness Muhammad is the messenger of Allah."

2. Accept the Qur'an as the criterion of truth and falsehood, justice and injustice, success and failure.

3. Accept the prophet Muhammad (may peace and blessings be upon him) as our role model.

LEARNING ISLAM

1. Learn the orthodox, traditional, and mainstream form of Islam (Sunni Islam) and avoid sects promoting any of the following heretical beliefs and actions:

    - To worship anything besides Allah (this is the biggest sin in Islam).

    - To believe Allah became a man (Allah never has nor will become a man).

- To believe there was or is another prophet after the prophet Muhammad (the prophet Muhammad was the final prophet; there won't be another after him, may peace and blessings be upon him).

- To hate, curse, or slander prophet Muhammad's companions (it's our duty to love and respect all the prophet Muhammad's wives, family members, and supporters).

- To distrust, hate, or kill all Muslims not part of their sect (Muslims are one community; dividing is a huge sin).

Plus, beware of people professing to be "holy men" or claiming to possess "secret knowledge."

2. Learn the simple, basic, and core Islamic fundamental that if Allah commands us to do something, then we do it how the prophet Muhammad (may peace and blessings be upon him) did it; and if Allah forbids us from doing something, then we don't do it.

3. Learn Classical Arabic for connecting with the Qur'an and other Muslims worldwide.

LIVING ISLAM

1. Worship Allah alone in both good times and bad because nothing has the ability or power to help or harm us except Allah; seeking help through magic, mystics, and lucky charms is disbelief.

2. Crave Allah's pleasure, fear His displeasure, and never lose hope in His forgiveness.

3. Unify our Muslim world (see Chapter 9).

9
FOR MUSLIM EYES ONLY: UNIFYING OUR MUSLIM WORLD

> *And the believing men and women are friends, helpers, supporters, and protectors of each other; they enjoin good, forbid evil, perform prayer, give charity, and obey Allah and His messenger; on them, Allah will have mercy: certainly, Allah is mighty, wise. Allah has promised the believing men and women gardens, with flowing rivers underneath, to live in forever, and beautiful mansions in the gardens of Paradise, but the greatest bliss is Allah's pleasure: that is the supreme success.*
>
> –The Qur'an 9:71-72 (translation)

Do you want to go to Paradise? Do you want your family, friends, neighbors, and as many Muslims as possible joining you in Paradise? This can happen only through a unified Muslim world. A unified Muslim world is Muslim-majority communities—bound together by love for Allah and His messenger (may peace and blessings be upon him), Islamic brotherhood/sisterhood, a common culture based on Qur'an and Sunna, and desire to fulfill Allah's order to be one ummah—forming a single political entity. Concentration is strength, and a unified Muslim world strengthens our ability to shape our world to our benefit:

- It empowers us to elect leaders that represent our principles, needs, and aspirations.

- It allows us to design societies in which worshiping Allah is natural, easy, and normal.

- It dramatically increases our opportunities for halal business, marriage, food, and entertainment.

- It enables us to defend ourselves robustly against all threats.

Today (1441 H), our Muslim world is divided and weak; we're abused by kings, strong-armed by dictators, oppressed by secularists, and bullied by kuffar. A few greedy elites, who have zero concern for Muslims' well-being, force themselves upon us and govern solely to loot, pillage, and exploit our Muslim communities. Our dignity, freedom, and rights are stolen; we're either prevented from worshiping Allah properly or hyper-strictness is shoved down our throats. We're boxed in, can't breathe, and don't know what to do. Banking and business can't be done without interest and bribery, unlawful sex is easier than marriage, and halal food and entertainment are difficult to find. Under these circumstances, going to Paradise is very difficult. The good news is it doesn't have to be like this; we can be unified, concentrated, and strong. Let's visualize how things can and should be. Imagine one political entity composed of every Muslim-majority community stretching from Morocco to Indonesia, open to the free worship of Allah, travel, trade, and marriage. Muslims choose their leaders, leaders govern for their citizens' benefit, everyone's free to pursue their dreams, and no one's stopped from doing anything unless it's undoubtedly haram. Classical Arabic is everyone's second language (making communication easy), zero-interest, bribery-free banking and business are the norm, marriage is easier than unlawful sex, and there's an abundance of halal food and entertainment. Sins are punished, but only open sins; hidden sins are left hidden and considered private matters between the sinner and Allah. Under these circumstances, our whole Muslim ummah's path to Paradise is clear, open, and in our hands. All this is doable, and it's how Allah wants us to live, we just need to make it happen: now. Unifying our Muslim world is a three-step process of committing to unifying our Muslim world, working to unify our Muslim world, and maintaining our unified Muslim world:

COMMITTING TO UNIFYING OUR MUSLIM WORLD

1. Make it our life's goal and invest the required resources (time, energy, money) to achieve it.

2. Acquire the necessary knowledge and know-how to make it happen, especially Qur'an, Sunna, and S.T.E.M. (science, technology, engineering, and mathematics).

3. Adopt a "victory or martyrdom" outlook because unifying our Muslim world won't be easy; we, our families, and our communities will be verbally abused, economically boycotted, physically harassed, imprisoned, tortured, raped, and killed; many individuals, or even a generation or two, will have to sacrifice themselves for the good of the Ummah; the reward, a unified Muslim world opening wide the path to Paradise for us all or the immediate enjoyment of the highest delights of Paradise due to our martyrdom, is definitely worth it.

WORKING TO UNIFY OUR MUSLIM WORLD

1. Unify locally, nationally, and internationally:

   - Each community elects a leader (ameer) for a single term (no second terms). The community pledges to obey all his decisions, especially concerning when the lunar months begin, when to perform the two Eed prayers, the prayer direction, and when to fight Jihad; Jihad is never fought without his permission. The ameer's decisions are disobeyed only when they're clearly haram.

   - Next, the ameers from neighboring communities come together and form a shura council and elect a leader for the collective communities; then, the ameers of collective communities come together and form a shura council and elect a leader for the region; this process is repeated until all Muslim communities are united under one leader (haleefa).

   - The haleefa appoints ambassadors to the various regions and communities to represent the central government and learn the people's needs, but the ambassadors don't govern.

2. Remove barriers to our unified Muslim world:

   - Get rid of the kings, dictators, secularists, and kuffar illegitimately ruling our Muslim world and replace them with elected leaders who represent our principles, needs, and aspirations.

- Replace both un-Islamic laws and overly strict interpretations of Islamic law with an orthodox, simple, and doable Islamic law based on Qur'an and Sunna and for the average Muslim's benefit.

- Eliminate from our heart un-Islamic ideas of racism, tribalism, nationalism, and sectarianism because they divide and weaken us. Allah commands us to love all Muslims like our family members and to be one unified Muslim ummah.

3. Resist those preventing us from unifying our Muslim world. It's our responsibility, our right, to live unified by Muslim principles; anyone opposing us is crushed.

MAINTAINING OUR UNIFIED MUSLIM WORLD

1. Maintain dedication to Islam because it's what binds us together; the minute another identity becomes more important than our Islamic identity or the difference between halal and haram becomes unimportant, our unified Muslim world will fracture.

2. Maintain fairness because communities and regions in our unified Muslim world that feel they're not getting their fair share, don't have equal access to opportunities, pay a higher price than the rest, or are treated like second-class citizens, will break away.

3. Maintain access to halal worldly benefits because though we're people desiring Paradise, we're currently living in this world and naturally pursue its halal delights. When the opportunities for halal travel, trade, marriage, food, and entertainment in other communities and regions of our unified Muslim world dry up, so does our enthusiasm for staying unified.

THE CLOSING

Remember Me and I'll remember you, be grateful to Me and don't disbelieve. O you who believe, seek help with perseverance and prayer; definitely, Allah is with those who patiently persevere.

—The Qur'an 2:152-153 (translation)

Beginning with promise
Full of high hopes
Falling face-first in the mud
Despite life's difficulties, I'm always moving on
Hardships spare no one
Bitterness and disappointment are frequent companions
High-stress and loneliness too
Even with their extra weight, I'm always moving on
Doing my best
Sometimes wrong, sometimes right
Many faults, mistakes, and sins
Making the good outweigh the bad
With Allah's help, I'm always moving on
Accepting the test
Embracing life's pleasures and sorrows
Through failure and tough times
Forgiving myself and hoping for better
Determined to persevere
Please Allah, I'm always moving on
Closing with no excuses or complaints
No blame, and no regrets

EJS 25 Rabee'ulAwwal 1441 (22 November 2019)

LIKE THIS BOOK? WRITE A REVIEW AT:
www.amazon.com

Made in the USA
Monee, IL
08 August 2024

63548920R00049